The Teacher Exodus

The Teacher Exodus

Reversing the Trend and Keeping Teachers in the Classrooms

Ernest J. Zarra III

ROWMAN & LITTLEFIELD
Lanham • Boulder • New York • London

Published by Rowman & Littlefield
An imprint of The Rowman & Littlefield Publishing Group, Inc.
4501 Forbes Boulevard, Suite 200, Lanham, Maryland 20706
www.rowman.com

Unit A, Whitacre Mews, 26-34 Stannary Street, London SE11 4AB

Copyright © 2018 by Ernest J. Zarra III

All rights reserved. No part of this book may be reproduced in any form or by any electronic or mechanical means, including information storage and retrieval systems, without written permission from the publisher, except by a reviewer who may quote passages in a review.

British Library Cataloguing in Publication Information Available

Library of Congress Cataloging-in-Publication Data Available

ISBN 978-1-4758-4370-5 (cloth : alk. paper)
ISBN 978-1-4758-4371-2 (pbk. : alk. paper)
ISBN 978-1-4758-4372-9 (electronic)

This book is dedicated to the next generation of teachers.
Generation Z awaits those of their own.

Contents

Preface		ix
Acknowledgments		xv
Introduction		xvii
1	Teacher Migration from Education	1
2	Fed-Up: Bureaucracy and Politics	23
3	Teachers Fighting for Change	45
4	Classroom Management and Teacher Support	65
5	Intervention, Training, and Retaining	85
Index		109
About the Author		115

Preface

This book originated as two chapters in my previously released book, titled *Assaulted: Violence in Schools and What Needs to Be Done* (2018). In many ways, this book can be considered the second in a series on teachers and their experiences in twenty-first-century classrooms. The decision was made to develop two books out of one manuscript. This was music to my ears and just another reason I enjoy the relationship with my publisher, Rowman & Littlefield.

The topic of teacher attrition is so vitally important to this nation and our students that it deserves examination of its own. Certainly, teachers are leaving the classrooms because of violence and threats against them. Although frightening in their own ways, there is much more to the story of teacher attrition than concerns about safety in the classroom. Thus, the primary reason for writing this book is to address many of the reasons for teacher attrition.

REASONS FOR WRITING THIS BOOK

In a general sense, *The Teacher Exodus: Reversing the Trend and Keeping Teachers in the Classrooms* is an overview of the many problems facing teachers today. However, more than an examination of the problems, this book has been written to delve into the specific reasons stated by teachers as to why they are leaving the profession.

School districts across this nation are advertising for teachers to fill classroom positions. Shortages are revealed each quarter. Students in many schools where there are teacher shortages are taught by emergency credentialed substitutes, or non-credentialed adults seeking employment.

The teacher shortage is real and so are the problems associated with the shortage. Both of these are particularly magnified in the cities and rural areas of our nation. Along with the teacher shortage, there is a secondary issue. This secondary issue relates to career longevity, which also impacts cities and rural areas.

Teachers are not sticking around in the career for as long as teachers had remained in previous generations. Teacher burnout is real. The stressors are real and very different than they were just a decade ago. For all the knocks that Millennials and Generation Z have taken over the years, they have resolved to choose other professions, rather than remain in one until burnout.

How does one encourage teachers to work in high-crime or dangerous neighborhood schools? Teachers seem to want to work in geographic areas where crime is low, academic achievement is known to be higher, and where the community supports the schools and teachers. I must admit, I wrote this book to challenge teachers to consider jobs in areas that are more challenging. My personal experience in a few difficult schools helped to shape my thinking about changes and reform. But more than this, those challenges taught me how to love people on levels below the surface.

THE INTENT OF THIS BOOK

The intent of this book is fourfold: (1) to bring to light the truth about why teachers are leaving the classroom, (2) to suggest ways to bring new teachers into the profession and motivate them to remain in the schools, (3) to encourage schools of education and teacher-training institutions to incorporate real-world training and experiences, across a wide array of districts and demographics, as to what to expect in today's public school classrooms, and (4) to cause elected officials and appointed bureaucrats to sit up and take notice about the culture that has been created by some of their decisions, and to consider changes to the environment created, which has sometimes led to diminishing and discouraging the passion of many of today's public school teachers.

OVERLOOKING SAFETY FOR EXPEDIENCY

As I wrote this preface, the Florida high school shooting was fresh on the minds of the nation. Contrast this with the fact that the 2018 Olympics are also in the headlines, and there is a very strange and surreal sense about our national priorities. Laws today favor students over teachers. Upcoming Supreme Court cases may revise or remove some of the teacher unions' hold on member dues.

Our nation is heading into the third decade of the millennium and it seems that individuality and personal expediency are of greater value than oneness and national unity. Overlooking issues in schools for personal expediency is, on the parts of policymakers, producing exactly what is intended.

Millennial and Generation Z teachers are not sticking around the classrooms in numbers that even come close to the previous generations of Xers and Baby Boomers. The value associated with commitment is being exchanged for job-hopping. Perseverance is traded for greener pastures, due in part to rapidly realized job dissatisfaction, and diminished emotional connections to the challenges for which they did not sign up. There are so many constraints on education and teaching, and less and less authority for teachers. That combination is a perfect storm for those without commitment and perseverance, or those who enter the profession with a good dose of these, but are tempered by the disappointments of the realities found in public education today

In my research, I discovered what many have long suspected about teachers at all levels. True feelings were primarily only spoken of in private, or in the school lounge. Lately, a growing number of teachers have been posting their stories on the Internet for all to read. Many are disgruntled, and some retire early. The bottom line is that a good number of teachers would actually call it quits, if not for the benefits, or the fact they have too many years invested in the job to give up and begin anew somewhere else.

WHAT IS SENSIBLE FOR KEEPING TEACHERS IN THE CLASSROOMS?

First, people must be attracted to the teaching profession. That is difficult enough, especially in the inner cities, as well as the more rural areas. If teachers are recruited and hired in these areas, there are problems in keeping them employed for many years.

Assuming school districts can actually attract people to their geographical location for employment, the question asked in the header of this section then becomes less difficult to answer. Given that, school districts must directly ask why teachers seek to remain in their classrooms and on their jobs. Jaws usually drop at the mention of this task.

There is the great fear that just asking the question might well cause teachers to think about leaving. Rather than hide in fear of the unknown, districts should personalize education, instead of relying on studies from the Hoover Institution, Pew, Gallup, or Rasmussen. Do districts really need to have data from hundreds of thousands of teachers to understand what is taking place in the minds and hearts of their own employees?

Reversing the current trend of teacher attrition can begin at the level of teacher training. Colleges and universities must do a better job at laying out the real world of the classrooms in which their students will be working. Observing in schools across the spectrum of public education is a must. Observing as many grade levels as possible is also a critical component to discovering if teaching is for the candidates, or not. Next, schools of education must worry less about their bottom line than placing good-to-excellent teachers into classrooms for careers. Therefore, professors should have candid talks with students about their motivation to become teachers.

I recall one such discussion in an introductory educational psychology class. I was challenging those seeking to become teachers and I asked a probative question about passion and motivation. One young man came up to me at the break and stated he was glad I asked this question. He decided that he did not have the requisite passion and desire to dedicate to teaching children and was glad he was able to decide to go a different route that very evening.

Another reason to consider if school districts are to keep teachers in classrooms is to allow them to teach students who want to learn and who are able to learn the necessary grade level standards, and curricular components established by the districts. Teachers are becoming so saddled with increasing numbers of special needs students, as well as newly mainstreamed students, that they are unable to achieve the best for neither the special students nor the regular education students.

Teachers of special needs students and special education students should be credentialed differently than regular education teachers. The trend today is to place as many "special" students as possible in the mainstream classes. Social activists have made their way into America's classrooms through the courts, and teachers did not sign up for the classroom teaching challenges they now face.

If politicians and education bureaucrats are intent on keeping the newer generation of teachers around for more than three years, they have to address forming new schools and better pull-out programs to meet the education needs of those with various special needs. Right now, these students are not being served. With diminished commitment already in the minds of younger teachers, school districts had better act quickly, or the migration of teachers away from the profession will continue its increase.

A third area that must be fixed for teachers to remain in the classrooms rests squarely on the shoulders of states and local boards of education. Teachers want to feel safe and they want their students to feel safe. The truth is that far too many teachers are experiencing physical violence, as well as violence against their reputations and against their property. Schools are naturally *soft targets* for large-scale events, such as Newtown, Connecticut and Parkland, Florida.

Added to this softness is the soft administration that now allows students to return to classrooms, rather than be sent home for violent outbursts and classroom disruptions. Teachers lack authority already, and to have a troubled student remain on campus, or return to class once he or she has settled down, only demonstrates that something other than safety underlies administrative actions.

WHY THIS BOOK IS IMPORTANT

This book is important because it gives a voice to teachers whose voices are usually shuttered, due to conflicts of interest, or unwillingness to state true feelings, so as not to look bad, or come across as unsupportive. This is just another hat worn by teachers and, while wearing it, their voices should be heard. What our nation should be listening to are the reasons teachers find it difficult to remain in the classrooms.

In some ways, leaving the profession they thought they loved and were committed to for a career is like a divorce. Teachers asking for assistance in the midst of their diminishing desire to remain employed as teachers, and their requests falling short of the attention of bureaucrats and administrators, do little to ameliorate the triggers for teacher attrition. This book may provide a necessary dose of reality to those whose attention is diverted for a political agenda or a reelection campaign.

This book is also important because of teacher attrition. Once teachers leave the profession, most do not return. While it is true that Baby Boomers are retiring, many others are retiring earlier than their predecessors.

Changes in culture, lack of discipline in students coming to schools, and a removal of teacher authority are drivers away from teaching for veterans who have lived through this slippage away from the profession they once adored. So, rather than work until their early-to-mid sixties, teachers are choosing to live on less money in retirement and to avoid all the changes that have resulted in less learning and more student-centeredness.

INSPIRATION FOR THIS BOOK

The inspiration for this book had its point of origin as I was writing another book. I began to read the words and stories of hundreds of teachers, listen to video testimonies of teachers who had left the profession, and perform my own informal survey. The anecdotes and data began to tell a sobering story.

Furthermore, as I read, images of my own children began to flash before me. I recall their teachers, the relationships built, and those who invested their own time and energy to ensure my children's success. Their years in school have made a tremendous difference in their lives to this day. Then I wondered whether their success could be realized today.

Such a shift in wonderment led me to more immediate thoughts of current students and not-so-recent memories of former students. Some very specific experiences came to mind, evoking some deep reflection and quietly expressed emotions. As adults, many of my former students are represented in every decade, from their teens into their mid-fifties, even serving as teacher to some of their children, and sharing friendship on social media pages.

In the midst of the memories and emotions, I thought about the moments in the past when I wondered if I had chosen the right profession. Was it going to be worth my time? Did I want to invest years in a profession that does not pay its employees well? Was such an investment a fit for my energies and my persona? What I realized is that I was asking the wrong questions.

The right question was do I want to affect lives and invest in humans and their futures? Teaching, after all, is the closest thing to parenting. These days there is greater leaning toward the latter, likely out of a sense of necessity for the well-being of students. I am grateful for those who treated my own children with the same love and respect they claimed to have treated their own children with. But this is not an essential for any great teacher.

What is essential is to be great enough to touch lives that will exponentially touch the lives of other generations. For whatever time I have left on this earth, I aim to continue the legacy of excellence laid out in the lives of my family and myself.

Acknowledgments

I want to thank all the teachers from my hometown of Bloomfield, New Jersey. From the moment I began Kindergarten at age four (no, it was not legal, but my parents got me in anyway) at Watsessing Elementary School, I have loved school. Mrs. Klein was so kind to me and always provided extra apple juice and graham crackers, if I took a nap on my rug.

From my earliest days, the memories of school are as vivid to me as if they happened nearly fifty years ago. Sarcasm aside, while walking the halls of South Junior High School, and then Bloomfield High School, where I was only one of over 700 graduates in the 1973 senior class, I have continued to love school.

The teachers in junior highs and high schools deserve acknowledgment, because I was a handful as a teenager. They deserve medals for working with teenagers and seeing to it that we received the best education possible, at that time. I remain deeply grateful.

After graduation, I headed off to spiritual boot camp at a Christian college, in Essex Fells, New Jersey. It was there that I met some of the people who would shape my young adult life—including my mate. At every step of the way, and in every school I attended, I loved school. It has now returned the love to me.

There is no irony, and there is certainly no surprise, in the fact that I am a teacher going on forty years in the classroom. I still love school.

So, on this page I acknowledge not only all the teachers who have touched my life, but the wonderful schools and the impact each of them had in my life.

To all teachers . . . thank you for your sacrifice on behalf of your students!

Introduction

The overarching purpose of this book is to serve as a complement to the book titled, *Assaulted! Violence in Schools and What Needs to Be Done*. In that book, I provide the reader with an understanding of a serious problem in schools today: increases in violence on school campuses. Solutions are also presented as a means to begin a serious examination of increased violence and deeper analysis.

In the book before you, *The Teacher Exodus: Reversing the Trend and Keeping Teachers in the Classrooms*, I explore the reasons (1) why students are not enrolling in teacher education programs like they did a decade ago, (2) why teachers are leaving their careers in the first three to five years, with veteran teachers also choosing to retire early, and (3) why there is a teacher shortage in almost every state. I have a heart for teachers and what they face each day. This book is a call for change on so many levels.

THE STRUCTURE OF THE BOOK

The book is five chapters in length and presents general and specific reasons for classroom teachers choosing to leave public school classrooms in America. Throughout the five chapters, there are many sections and subsections that will challenge the reader. Hopefully, as these issues are explored, the reader will come to understand the magnitude of the problems and the importance of some of the solutions offered.

Chapter 1 explores the depths of teacher migration from the classroom and the effects this migration is having on schools and teacher education programs. Teacher shortages have causes, and many of these causes are presented for the reader to examine. It is no coincidence that one of the main drivers of teacher exodus from schools is the issue of safety.

Education is at a tipping point in this nation and many are blaming the wrong persons. Along with teachers being blamed for many of the problems in schools, the issues of educational equity and what to do about the state shortages of teachers are presented.

Chapter 2 examines the roles of bureaucrats and politicians in shaping education policy and how that policy is shaped. The reader is also informed as to how to get the attention of elected officials for changes to be made in education. Along with this, restorative justice has a prominent place in the chapter as I consider *who bears the burden of accountability* in twenty-first-century American public schools. This chapter also contains a very important section on whether teachers are fearful of failing students, and the reasons they often do not give failing students the grades they deserve. I think the reader will be stimulated by this and other sections of this chapter.

Chapter 3 is about teachers standing up to fight for change. Education has become marginalized in the United States. There are roles and power structures for everything and everyone in education, and levels of importance assigned based on one level or another. Teachers are locked in to their profession, with little room to expand their expertise. Many teachers today cannot fathom a thirty-year career of doing the same thing, year in and year out.

Many teachers, rather than fight for change, are leaving the profession because they are being shamed and having to compromise their values. There is good news, though. Some states are making changes to support and protect teachers, and this is a good start. Rounding out the chapter is a hard look at mandatory expulsions and zero-tolerance policies against violence in schools.

Chapter 4 is the classroom management and teacher support chapter. Classroom behavior management strategies are presented and will prove helpful for newer teachers. There is a movement in America to view students as one demographic or another. Teachers are now being asked to teach with racial and ethnic understanding, and to see their students for their externals. Along with a discussion on this controversial matter, another is introduced: *Corporal Punishment*. The reader should find both of the topics quite engaging. All teachers will find help in the effective classroom management strategies presented and will come to understand their principals and administrators a little better.

Chapter 5 addresses intervention strategies, programs, and frameworks that seek to impact the modern American classroom. Along with these strategies, I include a section on specific intervention programs and their goals and purposes. Teacher training through professional development informs the reader that professional growth is important for the twenty-first-century public school classroom. Suggested behavior modification strategies are presented, with one of my own developed specifically for this book.

Introduction

At the close of each chapter, the reader will find sections containing recaps of the chapter and suggestions on how to reverse the trend of the teacher exodus in America. I trust the reader will find what he or she needs in order to be successful in a productive, rewarding, and long career in education. The education of our children is of paramount importance.

There are serious problems in our schools, as we know, and these problems are also found in our culture. We are losing far too many teachers, and not replacing them, with the exception of undertrained substitutes and interns. The hemorrhaging has to stop.

The takeaway for the reader is that this book will fairly assesses many reasons for our nation's current teacher exodus and suggests ways to end this migration, so as to ensure the education of the next generation of students in our nation's schools.

Chapter One

Teacher Migration from Education

> Many pre-service teachers aren't necessarily equipped with the skills to manage their classrooms. So, it starts with preservice education. This is a priority in special education, where teachers are really taught how to deescalate conflict.... Teachers cannot perform their job effectively if they feel threatened.[1]

Teachers are migrating away from teaching in public school classrooms across the nation.[2] Some of the teachers are retiring, but estimates in some states indicate that about 80 percent of those leaving the classrooms do so for reasons other than retirement. Some of the reasons for teachers choosing to leave the classroom include both personal and professional considerations.[3] Some of the personal considerations addressed below should raise concern in communities, so that action will be taken.

TEACHERS LEAVING THE PROFESSION

Some of the general, *personal reasons* teachers leave the classroom include[4] (1) personal safety, (2) economics and money, (3) lack of emotional support, (4) family time, (5) health and physical exhaustion, (6) time to retire, and (7) taking care of a family member.

Accompanying the personal reasons that teachers leave the profession are those that stem from a professional perspective. *Professional reasons* many teachers leave the classroom include:

- working conditions less than desirable
- lack of preparation for job assigned
- not allowed to fail students, due to philosophy that failure is not an option

- far too many hoops to jump through for students of diverse backgrounds and special needs to be able to meet needs of all learners
- lack of materials, including textbooks and technology
- students uncaring and apathetic
- parent threats and social media abuse
- tests and data have become as important as hungry, homeless, and unhygienic children
- toxic political climate
- unrealistic expectations placed on teachers
- unsupportive administrators
- pursuing further education, or professional positions outside education

All things considered, no one can be certain as to the blending of reasons that individual teachers end their careers. However, there are indicators of trends and patterns across states. In some cases, students are involved in forcing teachers to leave the teaching profession. Students have become wise to the inverted value of ruining someone's reputation and career through false accusations.

False Allegations and Accusations

Students are aware that false allegations toward teachers can lead to career and reputation ruination, as well as the breakups of families. In Maryland, abuse allegations affected the suburban Prince George's County, when "more than 500 school employees"[5] were placed on administrative leave. Since 2014, "cases of administrative leave have risen more than 600 percent."[6]

While the majority of reported incidents result in students being cleared of any commission of abuse, parents and students are somehow quicker today to make the claim of abuse at the notion that their child was touched, abused, or assaulted. Any physical touching, a mere look that is misinterpreted as uncomfortable, or the perception that a teacher is ignoring a student can result in false allegations.

Along these lines, of the 500 employees mentioned above, an estimated thirty percent of them "have been disciplined, and about 5 to 10 percent have been recommended for termination."[7] Regardless the truth, as to whether anything inappropriate actually occurred, allegations pertaining to any form of abuse are enough to derail a teacher's career.

Moreover, false allegations of the physical and sexual kind are those that become even greater concerns. These are concerns for all teachers. However, what is frightening to veteran teachers is that their careers and retirements could be placed in jeopardy by a vindictive person.

PUBLIC EDUCATION IS IN TROUBLE

Public education is at a tipping point and is in serious trouble in America. The range of problems in schools has reached new heights. The use of social media by adults, in ways similar to those used by their children,[8] is adding to the pressures for teachers and affects teacher retention. Most people seem aware today, in terms of the nation's focus on the problems and solutions associated with bullying.

The overwhelming focus of bullying in schools is from student-to-student, or group-to-student.[9] There are programs available to assist with problems associated with bullying. But are schools aware of the bullying that teachers endure? There are hardly any discussions regarding adults, or parents, who engage in assaulting teachers and teachers' characters, and those who are intent on sullying teachers' reputations by means of social media platforms.

Teachers Leaving the Classrooms

These are serious moments for teachers in America. Jason Allen writes, "The retention of teachers and staff is critical to the operations of schools. Schools that have a lot of resignations or transfers always indicate that something beyond the academics is wrong with the school. In fact, the majority of the morale issues are connected to the satisfaction of the teacher and staff."[10]

Teachers are leaving the profession in large numbers. Some of these teachers are leaving due to economic reasons and the inability to find housing in their areas. In some geographic regions of the nation, particularly in inner cities where housing in short supply, some schools are in such terrible condition that teachers fear for their safety. But the teacher shortage is as real as the housing shortage.

In California alone, the *School Boards Association Survey* shows that teacher shortages exist in three-fourths of the state's school districts. Also, "of the approximately 238,000 people who quit teaching after the 2011–12 school year—the most recent year for which data is available—almost two-thirds left for reasons other than retirement."[11] Housing expense is a concern, but definitely not the major concern surrounding teacher attrition.

Teacher Education Programs Affected

The numbers are pretty shocking. The number of people enrolled in teacher education programs around the nation "dropped from 691,000 to 451,000, a 35 percent reduction. . . . Fewer young people are interested in becoming teachers, and that's a problem because school enrollment is projected to increase by roughly three million students in the next decade."[12]

In areas where teachers are leaving the classrooms, the nation must come to grips with threats brought by students and their parents. Some of the reasons teachers are leaving are over threats to their safety as well as physical violence—and "they don't feel heard"[13] over many other issues. Ironically, in some cities, teachers previously restricted from classrooms are finding their ways back into the classrooms, even after allegations of misconduct.

Teachers' unions and bureaucrats are softening some of the restrictions of the past to work together to fill the classrooms with credentialed teachers who have a history of poor behavior. As in the case of New York City, the Department of Education reassigned previously removed subpar teachers from classrooms. Teachers were fired from schools and then forced upon principals at other schools, in order to fulfill teacher vacancies and absences. There was confusion over these actions as proponents believed they were witnessing a new form of social justice on behalf of the needs of students, while at the same time claiming such actions as far too risky, in placing bad teachers in front of students.[14] Apparently, allegations of the past are not as risky, or as important as filling classrooms in the present.

Policies and laws in public education today support the students over the teachers, especially if there is one or more specially protected category with which districts have been specially charged with lessening discipline referrals.[15] The reality is that if teachers are not safe their students are not safe. If schools are unsafe, then imagine the fears of families as they send their children off into such environments.

Frightening Examples

Families are left to wonder in Minnesota, after Como High School teacher Mark Rawlings was assaulted by two students. The district was slow in dealing with the assault.[16] Just a few months later, another teacher, John Ekblad, tried to break up a fight and was choked and body-slammed and lost consciousness. Ekblad still suffers from long-term residual physical ailments, such as numbness, vision problems, and headaches, according to his worker's compensation claim.[17]

Some Questions

Is a kindergartener's kicking of a teacher to be considered violence? How flagrant must an action be for the result to be considered an assault upon a teacher? Does a teacher have to fear a lack of safety for her and her classroom? Is being injured just part of the job, especially when working with students with special needs, on medication, or with violent home lives?

Accordingly, do violent actions have to be malicious and premeditated to constitute violence? At first, this may sound like a ridiculous question. Bureaucrats distant to the goings-on in America's classrooms must contend with such questions. Additional queries help to draw attention to the severity of the problem.

1. How are schools and teachers to understand students' impulses . . . as violent actions, or just happenstance incidents?
2. In terms of determining whether students are truly violent, must there first be a track record of such actions? How many actions equate to a track record?
3. Are patterns of previous years of violence reliable predictors of violence for the present and the near future?
4. If any injuries were to occur from an assault incident, would the injuries be enough to satisfy the definition of violence?

Education communities must answer these questions as they establish clear policies regarding students who are verbally abusive, hit others, throw objects at classmates, and even bully teachers. Bureaucrats need to find themselves closer to where the issues are in education. The only way to accomplish this is to make visits to their community's public schools to see for themselves.

Recipients of Violence

More and more teachers are on the receiving end of students actions that cause injuries. This places them (and their students) in unsafe schools and hostile classroom environments. They are subjected to the new gossip, which is social media enabled. Snapchat and Instagram allow posts and videos to disappear, and bring attention to "hit-and-run" online assaults. This advances the discussion and, out of necessity, forces revisits of the definitions of violence and assault.

Especially during this age of the Internet, the question must be asked as to whether a person has to know that he or she is harmed for an assault to be realized. Is it enough for others to understand that an assault has occurred? Reputations can be ruined online even before a teacher is aware of the impact upon his or her character and career.

Violence in Many Forms

School violence "takes on several forms and can include bullying, intimidation, gang activity, locker theft, weapon use, assault—just about anything that results in a victim."[18] The same should be true when teachers step in to assist students and promote campus safety. Teachers who are assaulted by students during student fights should be able to hold those students accountable for teacher injuries incurred. However, this is not often the case.

In 2017, at Mecklinburg High School in North Carolina, fighting students "ended up injuring a teacher"[19] when the teacher tried to break up a fight and was assaulted. The district states that "some teachers get trained on how to break up fights, but it is advised to let Campus Security Associates or other security step in."[20] The principal at the school called the fight "an altercation," and disciplined the students according to the district's code of conduct for students. No arrests were made even though during the previous 2016 school year, several personnel were also assaulted at this same school.[21]

At Cheltenham High School, which is in a suburb of Philadelphia, students were charged and one was arrested after a fight broke out that resulted in serious injuries to teachers. One teacher was knocked unconscious. "Eight teachers at a high school in Pennsylvania were injured while breaking up a brawl between four female students. . . . One substitute teacher suffered a concussion."[22] Another case that garnered national attention: "Kevin Straub, a St. Louis, Missouri, teenager, attacked his teacher so violently it triggered a stroke. The student was sentenced to 10 years in prison in 2014."[23]

Fights like these occur almost daily in American public schools, and often are recorded and posted to the Internet. Anecdotally, five fistfights broke out at the school at which this author is employed, on the very same day that this chapter was being edited. Social media was a major culprit in the assaults— one which involved a teacher and another which involved a security guard.

Students video their classmates causing brawls in their classes, as well as their classmates sometimes punching teachers.[24] But these fights are by no means relegated to only schools in the United States. According to an independent research team in the United Kingdom, "some 20 percent of staff working in schools said they were attacked by pupils or parents during the 2010–2011 academic year."[25]

AMERICAN CULTURE IS AT A TIPPING POINT

States under the Every Student Succeeds Act (ESSA) are taking advantage of advancing their more localized education policies and adopting new curriculum and standards. In some cases, these new adoptions have incorporated cultural changes, and many expect these changes to be part of classroom decorum, going forward.

For example, recent political actions are reasons for changes to *California's History-Social Science Curriculum Framework and State Standards*. The changes represent examples of interest groups affecting bureaucrats. California will now include in new social studies textbooks and curricula what some consider important historical contributions of those outside the mainstream of sexual identity and expression. Certain groups, often marginalized by society in the past, are now incorporated into certain states' curriculum, while others are left out.

Teachers that hold to the views of traditional marriage are now instructed not to assume students and their families abide by the traditional model of marriage and that it is offensive to some to speak of a mother and a father, or refer to students as male and female. Teachers are coming under scrutiny worldwide for not recognizing a student's personal claim of gender and sexuality, including references to genderless parents.[26]

Can the aforementioned actions be considered an assault on traditional American culture and upon teachers wishing to discuss the merits of a nuclear family, who must now exercise caution not to refer to genders and traditional relationships?[27]

Bureaucracy is handcuffing teachers of previous generations. Sociocultural changes do impact our schools and classrooms. More often than not, the Supreme Court must get involved, which can lead to even greater concerns,[28] depending on the political complexion of the court. Yes, sociocultural changes impact schools and students. Those who hold differing views on the newer cultural changes run the risk of being accused of all sorts of things. This includes teachers.

TEACHER SHORTAGES

The teacher shortage that is currently plaguing the nation is a result of several factors. Some teachers are retiring after storied careers. Others are retiring early, or are seeking employment in other professions. Still others choose to redirect their energies and walk away from the jobs they once enjoyed—and would still enjoy—if not for the changes in the system.

Teachers that enter the profession with unrealistic expectations, or an ideology of the world of education that is unchallenged by internship or student teaching, are often those who leave the profession within the first five years. There is an imbalance between expectations and reality. The statements one often hears from these teachers are, *Teaching is not what I expected when I got into it*, and *I did not feel supported by the administration when I had issues arise with students and parents*. Hence, the difference between expectations and reality.

The general consensus of those leaving the teaching profession is that they are leaving due to an overall disenchantment, not with the teaching profession, but with education as a whole. Teaching is a wonderful profession. Education bureaucracy, however, has a tendency to ruin teaching and is a major reason why teachers struggle to maintain passion for the profession.

The struggle experienced by teachers is validated by data drawn from a survey of education literature and the comments and personal anecdotes posted on the Internet. Teachers once reluctant to share openly the reasons they are struggling in schools are neither quiet nor reluctant as to the reasons they can no longer teach in America's public schools. Social media now empowers teachers to take to the Internet to share their concerns.

In Spokane, Washington, for example, public education is being hit hard by early resignations. The public schools of Spokane are "working hard to combat a troubling national trend" of teacher resignations. This trend is growing and has administrators very concerned.

For newer teachers, classrooms full of students for which they are not prepared and a lack of mentoring and professional support are major reasons for Spokane's mimicking of the national trend of teachers walking away from their classrooms during the year.[29] However, there are constraints placed on teachers today that are carryovers from the high-stakes NCLB era, and they persist even as the nation is currently within the parameters of the ESSA and more local control over education.

CONSIDERING THE CONSTRAINTS

Teachers are told their students are lagging behind and that test scores have to be raised. Consider the scenario that plays out across the nation in thousands of American public schools. Teachers are hired with the expectation that they will impact student learning, only to discover they are constrained by prepackaged restrictions placed upon them by the system.

One of the first constraints placed upon teachers comes by way of how they may be evaluated by students' assessment scores. Low test scores speak loudly. Another constraint placed on teachers seeking success is the realization of the disparity of vast student socioeconomic problems. The fact is that poor students and rich students do not have access to the same learning opportunities. Teachers are unable to fix poverty and they cannot be about diminishing a family's monetary value.

Third, teachers also find themselves constrained as they wrestle with the issues that arise from the fracturing of the nuclear family. These three constraints put together comprise a set of issues next to impossible to overcome. Left largely unaddressed in teacher training, these become real stressors in real classrooms, with real students.

Student Constraints

Students from all backgrounds and family structures are pulled in so many different directions, many times as a result of competing values from home, in the culture, and at school. Teachers face daily disciplinary concerns in classes with students who have emotional, behavioral, psychological, or any number of medical or mental health disorders. Students are pulled in many different directions these days.

Constraints are increased each time teachers are informed of a newly added district or school level curriculum. New academic programs, as well as assessments to evaluate students' and teachers' performances, still carry a lot of weight in this post-high-stakes era. Change for the sake of change brings instability. Irrational change does not provide sensibility. Students are always in the middle. Where does this leave American public education today?

Miracle Workers?

Common Core State Standards still persist in some states, even under ESSA. States that are exploring new ways to place untrained teachers in front of children must understand this practice is not a remedy to the growing problems associated with teacher shortages. It does not take long for untrained and newer teachers to feel overwhelmed by the varying degrees of educational expectations, especially under the remaining rigors of Common Core.

Teachers have this sense that they are expected to be near miracle workers, regardless of any limitations of resources. One expectation that teachers do not consider at the beginning of their careers is the amount of responsibility *and* subsequent blame placed on them. There is a difference in their ability to instruct in the very traditions that have formed much of society's stability in the past. However, things are different today. There is a strange irony applicable here: The problems are not of the teachers' making, yet the solutions are out of their reach.[30]

Rising Frustrations

Frustration levels rise in schools where students fall behind. Students fall behind for a variety of reasons. One of the reasons is the gap between student achievement and teacher expectations. When this gap widens, emotions take their toll and confidence tends to diminish. It is after this point that decisions are made by some students to check out of learning, and minds are made up by some teachers to leave the profession.

A recent phenomenon finds teachers are posting their letters of resignation online, as a means to offset the political or fictional reasons bureaucrats and administrators give for teachers leaving the profession. One teacher, Dr. Wendy Bradshaw, illustrates the frustrations of many teachers today:

> Like many other teachers across the nation, I have become more and more disturbed by the misguided reforms taking place which are robbing my students of a developmentally appropriate education. Developmentally appropriate practice is the bedrock upon which early childhood education best prac-

tices are based . . . the new reforms . . . are actively forcing teachers to engage in practices which are not only ineffective but actively harmful to child development and the learning process. . . . This letter is also deeply personal. I just cannot justify making students cry anymore. . . . Their shoulders slump with defeat as they are put in front of poorly written tests that they cannot read, but must attempt. . . . The children don't only cry. Some misbehave so that they will be the "bad kid" not the "stupid kid," or because their little bodies just can't sit quietly anymore, or because they don't know the social rules of school and there is no time to teach them. . . . The disorder is in the system which requires them to attempt curriculum and demonstrate behaviors far beyond what is appropriate for their age. . . . The disorder is in a system which has decided that students and teachers must be regimented to the minute and punished if they deviate. The disorder is in the system which values the scores on wildly inappropriate assessments more than teaching students in a meaningful and research based manner . . . my life changed when I gave birth to my daughter. I remember cradling her in the hospital bed on our first night together and thinking, "In five years you will be in kindergarten and will go to school with me." That thought should have brought me joy, but instead it brought dread. I will not subject my child to this disordered system, and I can no longer in good conscience be a part of it myself. Please accept my resignation from Polk County Public Schools.[31]

From Chained to Changed

The reality is that in many cases, due to unrealistic expectations placed upon them, teachers are finding their work less rewarding. Along with their work, administrative policies disallow holding students accountable for their behaviors and press teachers toward a quiet revolt, as they walk away from their positions. Thus, good and excellent teachers move on to other employment, or cease working altogether.

In the midst of all this, schools today seem much more concerned about progressive policies of inclusion and civil rights, and seem less concerned about teaching and learning.[32] For too long, the issue of teacher safety has been moved further down the list of education concerns. The time has come to change this, and a few states are doing just that.

BLAMING TEACHERS

Weak schools probably have weak administrators. Weak administrators tend to place blame on others, rather than on themselves. If administrators regularly observed the average classroom today, they would see classrooms that contain students with severe behavioral issues. They would also see teachers struggling to make sense of their environments, but making every effort to realize success each day.

Instead, many teachers are on the verge of exhaustion and anguish, just one step away from leaving the classroom altogether. Therefore, the most obvious conclusion to be drawn by any objective observer is that the teacher needs help with today's students. And who can blame them for seeking it?

Unfortunately, for teachers, these are the days when they find themselves blamed for so many things. Administrators criticize teachers for their supposed *poor classroom management skills*. This is unprofessional and inappropriate, and here is why. Teachers are not trained to deal with inordinate numbers of special needs students, now mainstreamed despite behavioral and emotional disorders.

If nothing else, teachers should be heralded as exceptional when they are able to keep the lid on their classrooms, given their current assignments and subsequent circumstances. If teachers are blamed for a lack of skill, then should administrators share the blame for the lack of leadership provided for teachers and the students in question?

Administrators blaming teachers for their poor classroom management skills must then also blame themselves for poor office management skills, should a student resort to behaviors that typify the actions that sent him or her to the office in the first place. Any administrator that deals with the same students sent to the office over and over again, knowing the possibility of such an *incident* happening again, is either inept or caught in a web of bureaucracy. Either way, teacher protections are far less than sufficient for today's classrooms.

The bottom line is if the same conclusions are drawn about the principal's handling of violent students, as are drawn about teachers' handling of these same students, then the world of education would treat teachers more fairly and think more often of their safety. If bureaucrats experienced what teachers' experience, then policies might change. There are double standards of expectations: one standard for teachers, and another standard for administrators and bureaucrats.

JUSTICE FOR PROFESSIONALS

The application of an administrative intervention strategy, applied by the principal on behalf of the teachers, might avoid second or third incidents of assault. No teacher should ever have to report a second physical assault of her person or have damaged property. It is bad enough a first assault occurred. Serious intervention should be provided after the first incident. Prevention of assaults should be first on the minds of those seeking justice for professionals, and this includes teachers and trained aides.

Thousands of American teachers in our nation's public schools are true professionals and deserve their own professional justice, as much as the students are deemed to deserve their social justice. Where are the policymakers lobbying for justice for the professionals in the classrooms around the nation? Why are teachers associations not calling for greater attention to this issue?

Arresting students is an intervention and deterrent for those who view assaulting adults as intolerable. Sometimes students do not fully understand the reasons for their actions. Their brains are not wired up to allow for the complete consequential understanding of their actions. Nevertheless, actions or behaviors need correction, reprimand, or both. That is also called learning, which is about what schools should be instilling for *the whole child*.

The first priority for teachers is to protect themselves and their students. This is professional justice. Programs for the adults that work at any school must be developed to deal with the rising problems of assault and violence against teachers, and these programs must address consequences. If they focus on the aspects of "why," over the actions that injure, more people will be injured in the process. Focusing on both is appropriate, but not at the moment of the assault. Again, no teacher should ever have to report being assaulted twice by the same student.

Following the Money and Education Entitlements

Funds should be allocated to develop safe classroom programs that focus on teachers. This is professional and just. The fact that the current Generation Z has the mindset that they are the center of the universe, provides little recourse in holding them accountable.[33] The amount of money spent on special needs students and special education is quite large, compared to the amounts spent on regular classroom students and teachers. States' numbers of dollars spent vary according to degrees of designations or the special categories that require funding. Teacher protections are not at the top of the list of funding priorities.

Parents generally know that special needs students get special attention. Special attention in education means special funds. Some of the most egregious and injurious assaults have been at the hands of students in districts where schools and parents have claimed special accommodations, because of the claims that these students were not given toward violence. Money does not necessarily create safe environments, but it does provide resources and people for classrooms to assist teachers. Nevertheless, despite the dollars, assaults still persist.

Finding a Safe Place

Anecdotes received during the research phase of this book are quite telling. For instance, imagine a classroom where students run to the corners, or hide under desks, when they know a student's anger is about to *explode*. Consider also students who are so traumatized and now accustomed to previous violent outbursts, that at the slightest hint of trouble, these trigger a screaming class to scurry about the classroom toward shielded safe places. This depiction is real and occurred at an elementary school.

In this depiction, there was a clear pattern of violence over time. There were multiple injuries sustained by adults and students as a result. Yet the administrator and district administrators did nothing to step in when asked to assist. Furthermore, to make matters worse, the teacher in question was unable, by law and district policy, to restrain the violent student.

In another instance, a teacher was instructed to remove her students from the classroom and call an educational aide to supervise a violent student's outbursts. The eight-year-old was undeterred, as he threw desks, chairs, pencils, and any other objects he could get his hands on. The teacher was not allowed intervene physically, under threat of a lawsuit. Eventually, a trained aide immobilized the arms of the student, and the violence and rage subsided. The aide was soon scrutinized and, as a result, stated she would never again use restraint on a violent student. In some schools, now even trained aides are constrained from protecting others.

Rather than be thrilled that their violent son had not injured more people during one of his outbursts, the parents' first concern was about the incident, and they directed a question to the aide: "Why did you touch my child?" Meanwhile, other parents questioned, "Why is violence allowed in the classroom, and why isn't the school doing something to protect our children?"

The reality is that policies and bureaucrats are often in the way of teachers. Another reality is that parents today tell their children not to take any bullying or sass from anyone and to fight back. There have been more than a few incidents of parents showing their children just how to handle a teacher with whom they disagree, with the children jumping on board the train of assault.

What's the Harm?

There are a few salient issues that are found between the lines of the incidents shared above. First, there is psychological distress experienced by students in the very places they are supposed to feel safe. Observing a teacher being injured, and watching rage take over a classroom, is quite frightening and even traumatic for children.

Second, personal experiences with panic yield quite an understanding of the impacts such threats and actions of violence have on the lives of children. Third, parents should be alarmed by such incidents, and so should school principals and administrators.

Many students in their own classrooms are psychologically harmed by outbursts of violent students. Likewise, when students witness an adult being injured by one of their own, the very person charged to protect them is compromised as unable to protect herself. This adds even more fear for students.

Bureaucrats do not seem to understand this point. Certain students have no business being in regular classrooms—especially if there is a track record of violent outbursts or injuries. They must be placed in alternative programs with lower teacher-student ratios, where the students would be able to be managed more effectively.

Is Equity Inequitable?

Would districts come to the support of teachers when parents threaten lawsuits for students' educational equity? Most likely not. The fact is that equity is less about teachers than about social and political issues involving students. This is exactly what has led to an increase in proposed legislation at the state level to try to regain some semblance of sensibility. But legislation does not go far enough in many instances.

One such example is Ohio, where a bill has been offered to protect students from violence, but has left teachers out of the equation. Along with student protections, "Teachers say they need to be protected as well, because currently, violence against them goes untracked."[34] Lawmakers in Columbus are reviewing ways to shore up teacher safety. Serious problems like these that occur in many schools today, and they occur at all grade levels.

Too many schools are quickly becoming places for arguments and fights, pedestals for racial and sexual expressions, and learning is suffering as a result of marginalization. Violence does nothing to promote unity, especially when it encroaches inward from the margins.

STUDENTS WITH SPECIAL DESIGNATIONS

The categories of special needs, the emotionally disturbed, and special education need to be carefully explained. Prior to the 2000s, special education programs expanded and state programs incorporated a host of titles of additional disabilities, disorders, and syndromes, into which students fit within the Americans with Disabilities Act.

Today's education climate takes the individual student and classifies the student under a blanket of classifications, focusing less on behaviors and more on the *causes* of behaviors. These students are mainstreamed into regular education classes. Many of these students might have fallen under the special education umbrella in the past, given their low achievement, or poor reading ability on assessment results.

Sometimes students with special needs lash out and injure others, yet little to nothing is done to help these students. The laws in more progressive states allow these students extra leeway in classrooms. In many states, due to lawsuits, parents have fought successfully to enroll their special needs children in regular classrooms.

This presents a serious dilemma for teachers. So many teachers are in a quandary about their careers, due to the increases of special needs issues that are distracting from the educational processes for all students. Such distractions do little to encourage teachers toward career longevity.

THEORY OR REALITY?

Theories make excellent intellectual conversation. But when parents, educational professionals, office staff, teachers and students witness near-daily emotional outbursts and acts of violence, what then? We live in more than the theoretical. With the changes within the politics of the United States, one can be called a "racist" for suggesting to make schools safer by seeking solutions that exit troubled and violent students from their schools and place them into alternative programs.[35] This is not a theoretical accusation. The accusation is real. The question is, how did our nation arrive at this juncture?

Disparate Impact Theory

Under the *disparate impact theory*, put into place by the Obama Administration, even sending a student to the office for being abusive by not complying with school cell phone policies can land a person and a school in a discrimination lawsuit.[36]

Every district now cowers in fear over the possibility of being labeled racist.[37] It is precisely because of these fears that teachers are feeling less safe in their roles. Feeling less safe is not an incentive for teaching and learning, another fact that escapes our nations' leaders.

What also must be called into question is a public education system that appears to protect special needs students over teachers and all other students in classrooms. Districts have no intervention programs to deal with violent students, let alone violent special needs students. Laws and subsequent legal worries from their enforcement are often constraining, as the state of Texas points out.[38]

The majority of teachers are not special education experts, yet they must deal with what only experts could expect. Sometimes even the experts are surprised by behaviors of their special needs students. What have schools come to that they are havens for drug babies, drugged students, bipolar teens, the ADHD accommodated, autistic, and low achievers who may also be emotionally and psychologically disabled? Likewise, students come to school these days full of anxiety disorders, emotional and behavioral disorders, learning disabilities, and medication.

Many students today are seemingly angrier over the smallest of issues. Social media has not helped to diminish any of these conditions, and allowing cell phones to be used throughout the entirety of the school day is not a *smart* idea. Does this sound like public education is headed in the right direction?

THE ROLE OF RACE

The term racism is tossed around in the media by race-baiters and provocateurs so often that much of its intended sting has been lost on the ears of the average American. Such labels drive teachers away from teaching, and that is a shame. Real racism still exists, but the message has become expedient for political purposes and is used as an accusatory label. Rather than draw attention to serious racial divisions and problems in schools, demagoguery has often impeded the message, leaving students in the lurch. Good teachers are offended by accusations against them, especially when skin color is associated with the accusation.

As a nation, we cannot dismiss that race is a very hot topic, politically and socially. There is much to be gained by certain groups in the debate on racial equality, but is it best to continue to focus on points of inequality? Focusing always on the past or differences is contrary to focusing on restoration and growth. Does social justice always focus on past injustices as if nothing has changed in the nation? It certainly seems to be the case.

The regular opening of old wounds does nothing for the healing and overall health of education for today's students. Why subject an entirely new generation of students to what plagued our national morality decades ago? Some refuse to acknowledge this approach.

Critical Race Theory

There is a groundswell of concern about race that is not the typical lambasting found so often in the American media. This concern is centered on Critical Race Theory (CRT) and takes race to an entirely new level of national consciousness. Although it has been around for some time, its rebirth in the psyches of Americans is worth noting.

Critical Race Theory espouses that whiteness is a property. The interests of blacks in America, and other people of color, in achieving racial equality will be achieved only at points of convergence with the interests of whites who are in positions to affect and change policy.[39] Furthermore, CRT also emphasizes that racism is such a deeply ingrained and endemic part of the American fabric that it can be found both consciously and subconsciously in most every facet of the American way of life. The notion is that CRT thinking is so pervasive and endemic to American culture that it affects the "economy, schools, government,"[40] and the common, everyday person.

Essentially, CRT suggests that "things must be made unequal in order to compensate for that racism."[41] The way this theory plays out in schools, as well as in the criminal justice system, is "when a Black student is disruptive ... it is not their fault."[42] This is the ultimate in focusing on differences, while calling for equality.

It is Critical Race Theory, and the application of this theory, that has one black teacher in the St. Paul, Minnesota Public School District bringing a federal law suit against the district. Aaron Benner spoke up about an Obama-era program that "forced school districts to address disproportionate percentages of minority students being suspended for bad behavior."[43] Benner's main concern about this program was that "the data was being manipulated to keep the numbers low for behavioral referrals when in reality they were going up.... That's fraud and unethical."[44]

This all came to light when Benner was punched by a student, "and the student was sent back to the classroom within minutes, without any disciplinary action taken."[45] Under Critical Race Theory, it is underlying racism, and not a student of color or his or her actions, which are truly responsible for all of a person's behaviors.[46]

Therefore, the fact that a black teacher was punched by a black student is concluded to have been caused by a fundamental, underlying racism in America. How can teachers ever overcome such stereotypes, in order to assume positions of authority in classrooms containing students from various demographics? This cannot help but lead to higher rates of attrition among teachers.

Teachers are at a loss as to how to deal with the racial marginalization that has become very much a part of American culture and effects learning on a daily basis. It seems so many things act as triggers to set off emotions. Even classroom rigor has been criticized as a cause of turmoil, backlash, and violence.

Is Rigor a Trigger for Special Needs Students?

With mainstreaming and inclusion programs, how could any teacher or parent expect rigorous and challenging learning environments to succeed today? There is no fairness to those students to place them in environments where they cannot learn and are sometimes triggered by their peers and their surroundings. Fearful or angry regular education students do not make good learners and may be only moments away from demonstrating their own frustrations and adding to the issues already in the mix.

Today, special needs students now garner special protections in public schools. Yet those not designated with special protections are the teachers. Special needs students may be quicker to react negatively to situations involving rigor and react with extreme emotions. They may be unable to see beyond the emotional moment, or simply do not perceive what is actually occurring within a larger context. In this sense, many students may need to be coached to filter their emotions and practice self-control.[47]

Special education teachers usually major in specific areas of *special education* to work with "special needs" students. Regular education teachers are not trained to work with special needs populations. Most teachers do not go into education to work with special needs students. Such assignments are deep, soulful callings. That being said, teachers are usually a compliant group, and they take their classes as they are assigned to them, hoping to make a difference with each student.

REVERSING THE TREND

There are several things that stakeholders must consider, and even support, if they intend to reverse the exodus of teachers from classrooms across America. First, teachers must be trained and qualified to assume their positions as teachers. Far too many are given the title *teacher*, but lack the proper education, complete certification by a state, and fall short of the refinement of their skill sets needed to work with today's students.

Second, administrators must communicate and demonstrate that they have the backs of their teachers and persons filling classrooms. If a person carries the title of *teacher*, administrators must respect the title and be in support of the efforts of the faculty. Third, serious concerns exist today for teachers and the levels of abuse they incur from students and parents. No teachers should ever have to go to work fearing for their safety or that by doing their jobs they will be ruined on the Internet.

It is clear that teachers do not want to spend a lifetime dealing with emotional and physical abuse—especially when their actions against such matters are constrained by laws and bureaucratic policies. If teachers are to be retained and productive, then these matters must be addressed with some semblance of progress toward resolution.

Fourth, blaming and shaming of teachers by administrators has to cease. Administrators taking responsibility for matters is the professional thing to do. Placing blame where it does not belong is not only unethical, it reflects pettiness and a serious lack of professionalism. These actions are not convincing teachers to continue their careers well into their futures.

Administrators must support their teachers. In the final analysis, which teachers feel they can work for an administrator, when the administrator feels the faults associated with students' behaviors are the teachers' own doing? Reversing the trend of teacher exodus will never be accomplished by blame and shame.

Lastly, states must begin viewing education from the perspective of academic value, rather than social value. Schools are not agencies by which factions can engineer and mobilize student cohorts toward one social issue or another. The divide in culture is deep enough. It should not be made worse by efforts to please all factions in education. Actions such as these are likely driving many from their passionate pursuits in the classrooms as teachers.

Our nation should take seriously the training of teachers. Bureaucrats and politicians must join in the support. America should *train to retain*, and not just *train to place* into jobs for the moment. Since veteran teachers are the backbone of any school, they should be queried as to ways to assist in keeping teachers *at home* in the local schools. Newer teachers would benefit greatly from the corporate wisdom and learn reasons why they should stay in the profession, rather than leave at the first chance they get.

NOTES

1. Tim Walker. "Violence against teachers—an overlooked crisis." *NEA Today*. February 19, 2014. Retrieved from http://neatoday.org/2013/02/19/violence-against-teachers-an-overlooked-crisis-2/.

2. Liz Riggs. "Why do teachers quit: And why do they stay?" *The Atlantic*. October 18, 2013. Retrieved from https://www.theatlantic.com/education/archive/2013/10/why-do-teachers-quit/280699/.

3. Eric Westervelt and Kat Lonsdorf. "What are the main reasons teachers call it quits?" *NPR Education*. October 24, 2016. Retrieved from http://www.npr.org/sections/ed/2016/10/24/495186021/what-are-the-main-reasons-teachers-call-it-quits.

4. Alex Thomas. "Why teachers quit." *The Best Schools*. April 5, 2017. Retrieved from https://thebestschools.org/magazine/why-teachers-quit/. See also Dick Startz. "What do teachers do when they leave teaching?" *The Brookings Institution*. May 9, 2016. Retrieved from https://www.brookings.edu/blog/brown-center-chalkboard/2016/05/09/what-do-teachers-do-when-they-leave-teaching/.

5. Donna St. George. "Abuse allegations lead to spike in teachers placed on leave in Maryland suburb." May 7, 2017. *The Washington Post*. Retrieved from https://www.washingtonpost.com/local/education/abuse-allegations-lead-to-spike-in-teachers-placed-on-leave-in-a-maryland-suburb/2017/05/07/0014c8ac-26d5-11e7-b503-9d616bd5a305_story.html?utm_term=.b5d19a216d93.

6. Ibid.

7. Ibid.

8. Taylor Hatmaker. "A huge survey shows that teens are bullied most on Instagram and Facebook." *Tech Crunch*. July 20, 2017. Retrieved from https://techcrunch.com/2017/07/19/ditch-the-label-2017-cyberbullying-report/.

9. Robert Preidt. "Bullying takes financial toll on U.S. school districts." *Health Day*. July 6, 2017. Retrieved from https://consumer.healthday.com/kids-health-information-23/bullying-health-news-718/bullying-takes-financial-toll-on-u-s-school-districts-724168.html.

10. Jason B. Allen. "Teacher morale impacts achievement." *EdLanta*. December 8, 2017. Retrieved from http://edlanta.org/teacher-morale-impacts-achievement/.

11. Stephen Wall. "Is housing built for teachers a solution to California's staffing shortage?" *Press Enterprise*. July 2, 2017. Retrieved from http://www.pe.com/2017/07/02/bill-would-help-pay-for-teacher-housing/.

12. Patrick J. Kearney. "Where are all of the teachers going?" *Huffington Post*. July 16, 2017. Retrieved from https://www.huffingtonpost.com/entry/where-are-all-of-the-teachers-going_us_596b7e10e4b06a2c8edb474c.

13. Ibid.

14. Staff. "City hall's rush to put bad teachers back in the classroom." *New York Post*. July 10, 2017. Retrieved from http://nypost.com/2017/07/10/city-halls-rush-to-put-bad-teachers-back-in-the-classroom/.

15. Juanita Chavez. "Historic settlement reached in lawsuit against Kern High School District, 7/26/17." *Dolores Huerta Foundation*. August 11, 2017. Retrieved from http://doloreshuerta.org/historic-settlement-reached-in-lawsuit-against-kern-high-school-district-72617/.

16. Editorial Board. "If teachers aren't safe, students aren't safe." *Star Tribune*. March 11, 2016. Retrieved from http://www.startribune.com/if-teachers-aren-t-safe-students-aren-t-safe/371846501/.

17. Josh Verges. "St. Paul teacher's lawsuit over Central High assault dismissed." *Twin Cities Pioneer Press*. May 25, 2017. Retrieved from http://www.twincities.com/2017/05/25/ekblad-judge-dismisses-st-paul-teachers-lawsuit-over-central-high-assault/.

18. Dorothy Espelage, Eric M. Anderman, Veda Evanell Brown, et al. "Understanding and preventing violence directed against teachers." February–March 2013. *American Psychologist* 68, no. 2, 75–87 (viz. p. 76).

19. Dedrick Russell. "Teacher assaulted while breaking up fight involving students." *WBTV Charlotte*. April 28, 2017. Retrieved from http://www.wbtv.com/story/35279312/video-teacher-assaulted-while-breaking-up-fight-involving-students.

20. Ibid.

21. Ibid.

22. Stephanie Haney. "Eight teachers are injured after trying to break up wild girl fight caught on video in high school hallway." *Daily Mail*. May 4, 2017. Retrieved from http://www.dailymail.co.uk/news/article-4474772/Eight-teachers-injured-trying-break-wild-girl-fight.html.

23. Editorial Board. "If teachers aren't safe, students aren't safe." *Star Tribune*. March 11, 2016. Retrieved from http://www.startribune.com/if-teachers-aren-t-safe-students-aren-t-safe/371846501/.

24. Rebecca Klopf. "Video shows Milwaukee teen punching teacher." *ABC News*. August 22, 2017. Retrieved from http://www.tmj4.com/news/national/milwaukee-teen-arrested-for-punching-teacher-1.

25. Graeme Paton. "One-in-five teachers have been 'physically attacked' at school." *The Telegraph*. September 2, 2011. Retrieved from http://www.telegraph.co.uk/education/educationnews/8735837/One-in-five-teachers-physically-attacked-at-school.html.

26. Martha Azzi and Nelson Groom. "Schools banned from using the terms 'mum and dad' and boys told to dress up as girls in 'non-gender-specific free play.'" *Daily Mail Australia*. July 20, 2016. Retrieved from http://www.dailymail.co.uk/news/article-3699679/Schools-banned-using-terms-mum-dad-boys-told-dress-girls-non-gender-specific-free-play.html. Cf. Staff. "He? She? Ze? Colleges add gender-free pronouns for students." *CBS News*. September 18, 2015. Retrieved from https://www.cbsnews.com/news/harvard-university-colleges-gender-free-pronouns-transgender-genderqueer-students/.

27. Ryan Dailey. "Teacher requests students use gender-neutral pronouns: Parents divided." *USA Today*. September 20, 2017. Retrieved from https://www.usatoday.com/story/news/nation-now/2017/09/20/teacher-requests-students-use-gender-neutral-pronouns/687647001/. See also Todd Starnes. "NC school to teachers: Don't call students 'boys and girls.'" *Fox News*. August 16, 2016. Retrieved from http://www.foxnews.com/opinion/2016/08/16/nc-school-to-teachers-dont-call-students-boys-and-girls.html.

28. Kate Shellnutt. "Christian orgs labeled hate groups on top charity site." *Christianity Today*. August 24, 2017. Retrieved from http://www.christianitytoday.com/news/2017/june/christian-charities-labeled-hate-groups-guidestar-splc-frc.html.

29. Rob Harris. "Spokane public schools looks to reduce new teacher resignations." *KREM*. November 13, 2017. Retrieved from http://www.krem.com/news/education/spokane-public-schools-looks-to-reduce-new-teacher-resignations/491446517.

30. Staff. "Teacher resignation letters paint bleak picture of US education." *Phys.Org*. April 6, 2017. Retrieved from https://phys.org/news/2017-04-teacher-resignation-letters-bleak-picture.html.

31. Valerie Strauss. "Special ed teacher quits: 'I just cannot justify making students cry anymore.'" *The Washington Post*. October 25, 2015." Retrieved from https://www.washingtonpost.com/news/answer-sheet/wp/2015/10/25/special-ed-teacher-quits-i-just-cannot-justify-making-students-cry-anymore/?utm_term=.381ae73a79f3.

32. Brenda Iasevoli. "Teachers go public with their resignation letters." *Education Week*. April 14, 2017. Retrieved from http://blogs.edweek.org/edweek/teacherbeat/2017/04/why_do_teachers_quit_their_res.html.

33. Ernest J. Zarra, III. *The entitled generation: Helping teachers teach and reach the minds and hearts of Generation Z*. Lanham, MD: Rowman & Littlefield, 2017.

34. Paul Orlousky. "Proposed bill aims to protect teachers against violence in schools." *Cleveland 19*. Retrieved from http://www.cleveland19.com/clip/13147383/proposed-bill-aims-to-protect-teachers-against-violence-in-schools.

35. Paul Sperry. "You're now a racist if you say schools need to be safer." *New York Post*. April 10, 2016. Retrieved from http://nypost.com/2016/04/10/youre-now-a-racist-if-you-say-schools-need-to-be-safer/.

36. Ibid.

37. Ibid.

38. Denise Hays. "Dangerous students in the schools: A legal perspective on sharing information or not." *Walsh, Anderson, Gallegos, Green, and Trevino: Attorneys At Law*. n.d. Retrieved from http://www.txasp.org/assets/conference-materials/2014/dangerous%20students%20in%20the%20schools%20handout.pdf.

39. Richard Delgado and Jean Stefancic. *Critical race theory: An introduction*. 3rd edition. New York, New York: New York University Press, 2017, pp. 8, 14, 22, passim. See also Adrienne D. Dixson. "What is critical race theory in education?" *The Ohio State University Summer Institute* and *The Metropolitan Center for Urban Education at New York University*. July 19, 2007. Retrieved from https://steinhardt.nyu.edu/metrocenter.olde/programs/TACD/Summer%20Institute/SummerInstitute2007/powerpoints/CriticalRaceTheoryandEducation.pdf.

40. Caleb Parke. "Black Minnesota teacher says district discriminated against him for questioning race-based programs." *Fox News*. October 12, 2017. Retrieved from http://www.foxnews.com/us/2017/10/12/black-minnesota-teacher-says-district-discriminated-against-him-for-questioning-race-based-programs.html.

41. Ibid.

42. Ibid.

43. Ibid.

44. Ibid.

45. Ibid.

46. Adrienne D. Dixson. "What is critical race theory in education?"

47. Staff. "Symptoms and accommodations." *Juvenile Bipolar Research Foundation*. n.d. Retrieved from https://www.jbrf.org/page-for-families/educational-issues-facing-children-with-bipolar-disorder/symptoms-and-accomodations/.

Chapter Two

Fed-Up

Bureaucracy and Politics

> Many students are just not ready for a regular school because they have personality disorders, anger management issues, learning disabilities, lack of respect for authority, inability to concentrate (ADD), and other issues that Alternative Education has been dealing with for years, and knows how to go about it.[1]

All across the United States, schools are succumbing to lawsuits in the name of educational equity. This means students who would never have been placed in a regular education classroom just a few years ago are now being included in greater numbers in regular education programs.

Inclusion is a new education buzzword, and it means a lot of things for twenty-first-century schools. Education, as a whole, must take care not to be so politically correct that it stimulates educational ineffectiveness. Educational ineffectiveness is described as trying to be all things, to please all people, so that mediocrity is the highest outcome achievable.

Jane Meredith Adams exemplifies this concern, when it comes to dealing with violent students. She writes, "As California presses school districts to stop suspending hundreds of thousands of students a year, many teachers . . . say they have been under-prepared for the change, according to a new survey by the California Teachers Association. . . . Nearly 8 out of 10 teachers surveyed said they need more training and the support of school psychologists and counselors if they are to successfully retreat from 'zero tolerance' discipline practices, in which even minor infractions may result in a student being sent home for a day or more."[2]

EDUCATIONAL EQUITY AND RESTORATIVE JUSTICE

In terms of restoring violent students to their classrooms, President Eric Heins believes, "Restorative and positive practices are the right direction to go . . . referring to restorative practices that allow students to make amends and to programs that teach positive social and emotional skills and provide counseling and other interventions."[3] However, what is being discover is that "students are being thrown back into the classroom and nothing has been done to deal with their behavior. . . . Eighty-six percent of nearly 3,500 teachers and other school staff who completed an online survey between May and December 2016 said they need additional training in how to reach the students they once may have sent to the office, as well as increased access to school mental health professionals to support students in distress.[4]

Some of the comments by California teachers, which were posted to the Adams (2017) article, indicate that not all CTA members and non-members that are in the classroom agree with the direction the state board of education is headed. Likewise, the same sentiments are applicable to some in leadership at the CTA. Observe the following sample comments:[5]

- "I am thankful this is my very last year of teaching in California. The infinite wisdom of Sacramento strikes again. I as a teacher am supposed to allow some malcontent to disrupt the learning environment and sabotage everyone else's education. What would the politicians do to a disrupter who tried to sabotage their legislative process? Why have them removed of course. More double standards as usual." (Dave)
- "Developmental trauma changes the architecture of the physical brain, ability to learn and social behavior. It impacts 2 out of 3 children at some level, but I didn't even know what it was." (Daun)
- "Seems that most any problem, whether educational, psychological, socioeconomic, or medical, can apparently be solved by having trained teachers receive more training and sit through more seminars." (Raoul)
- "For a school to work, a student must adhere to a modicum of basic behavior guidelines without which the class cannot proceed with learning." (Don)

Who Bears the Burden of Accountability?

One of the problems with placing the brunt of suspensions and expulsion reductions on teachers is that this places them on the front line of accountability. Who or what is helping parents to hold their own kids accountable for their actions? Why is it the school's responsibility to correct behaviors that originate at home? Why should teachers act as the parents of their students?

Teachers are not trained in psychotherapy. Most took a limited number of psychology classes in undergraduate and credential programs. Teachers are nominal behavior modifiers for large groups, and not behavior controllers. Students must learn to self-regulate and control their own behaviors.

Self-regulation is difficult for students when there are few effective filters, little knowledge of weak discipline policies, and multiple poor behavior trigger points that exist in classrooms. Students do not necessarily need incentives to misbehave. But give them some incentives through perceived weakness, and stand back.

Parents must teach self-control to their children, first and foremost. If not, then students who are unable to control their behaviors should be removed from the environment until they can control themselves. Actions without consequences teach the wrong message, both at home and in school.[6] The school can offer assistance but should never usurp the role of the parent.

State education codes and school district policies make it very difficult for teachers to gain protections against being assaulted in class. First, the use of self-defense may result in being fired. Second, injuries inflicted upon students are actionable and parents most likely would bring legal action. Third, the laws are written to protect students. Education codes complicate matters, either by being convoluted or by missing the point.

For example, the education code for the state of New York states that a principal may suspend a student in elementary through high school for up to five days for violations of the code of conduct. The violations include the following:

> (a) commits an act of violence upon a teacher, administrator or other school employees; (b) commits, while on school district property, an act of violence upon another student or any other person lawfully upon said property; (c) possesses, while on school district property, a gun, knife, explosive or incendiary bomb, or other dangerous instrument capable of causing physical injury or death; (d) displays while on school district property, what appears to be a gun, knife, explosive or incendiary bomb or other dangerous instrument capable of causing death or physical injury; (e) threatens, while on school district property, to use any instrument that appears capable of causing physical injury or death; (f) knowingly and intentionally damages or destroys the personal property of a teacher, administrator, other school district employee or any person lawfully upon school district property; or (g) knowingly and intentionally damages or destroys school district property.[7]

If a student is suspended in the 2000s, there are four steps that need to be taken by the building principals. "Step 4 states: School authorities must arrange for the student to receive alternative instruction (if the student is compulsory school age). . . [a] Minimum one hour of alternate instruction per day for elementary students; Minimum two hours of alternate instruction per day for secondary students."[8]

Anyone can see the many bureaucratic hoops one must jump through and the number of accommodations necessary before a student can be disciplined. How many opportunities does a teacher get for his or her *mistake*?

INEQUITY OF A DIFFERENT KIND

A student can commit some very serious assaults, use weapons, and even cause death, in rare cases, and sometimes be restored. In New York, the New York Board of Education requires alternate instruction for the student on the part of the school. Students, as the very center of the education universe, have most of the rights and protections today. In some states, many special education students may continue to be matriculated until age twenty-one, or older. These policies are not uncommon in the United States.

The expression of an individual, or a faction, is now the favored point of focus in much of education. Teachers are told not to correct any student expression, but to facilitate and validate their expression, as students begin to own who and what they are. The student is the "center" of education, which continues to erode and disable the teacher from the position he or she once occupied in the classroom.

Bureaucracy has now made it possible for teachers to be class monitors and education facilitators, rather than teachers in American public schools. Students are now supposed to be the decision makers over their own learning and hold themselves accountable. (See figure 2.1.) The issue that arises from the practice of this philosophy is that fewer students are demonstrating their learning of self-control in significant or tangible ways.

Figure 2.1 points out how education has flipped in placing the student at the center of the education hierarchy as the *merry monarch*. The student now calls the shots and the recipients are often rendered helpless, as they recognize the centrism of the student.

DISPARITY IN TREATMENT

While today's students are given the lion's share of protections and chances to succeed, teachers are usually given one chance and then they are disciplined harshly. Usually teachers are fired or reassigned away from students, after an action that goes against policy or violates the law. As the policy goes, teachers are the professionals and should always know better. However, what about non-professional teachers, those working on emergency credentials, or the non-credentialed?

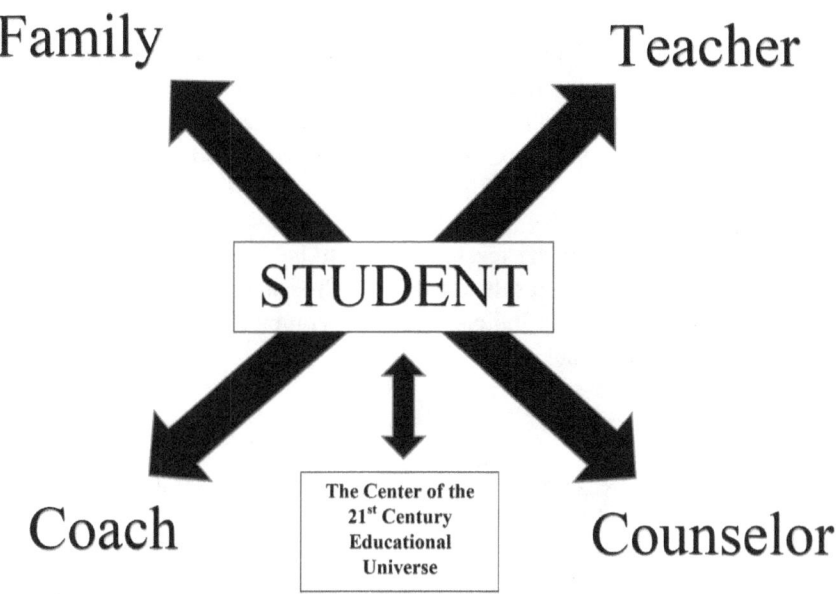

Figure 2.1. Model of Student Centrism

One of the problems with this is the multiplication of non-credentialed teachers that are showing up in districts all over America, and at all levels. These folks are not trained to handle many of the situations they may face in public schools. Interns learn on the job and often with minimal support.

Teacher shortages are exacerbating the problems within the classrooms. Substitutes that replace regular teachers are not necessarily trained educators, but they are filling a gap. Likewise, older retirees from different generations returning to the classroom see the world very differently than Gen Z students. There is an ever-increasing disparity between teachers and students in classrooms.

There is also great disparity in the ways teachers are treated, as opposed to the ways students are coddled. Some of these disparities are directly the result of political power and state-level education decisions. Another reason is because of the culture in America, which has become more tolerant of so many types of behaviors.

Removing Teachers

Teachers are removed from classrooms all over this nation for inappropriate behaviors with students. Crude jokes, or innocently touching a student, are enough reasons to discipline teachers. Teachers must be extra careful today. Students are held to a set of different standards.

Students know that teachers are essentially powerless to force them to do anything, and sometimes bait them into actions. Some teachers cross the lines of propriety with students by premeditation, or predation, which are other issues unto themselves. Please refer to the book *Assaulted! Violence in Schools and What Needs to Be Done* for additional discussion on these matters.

Anyone entering into the teaching ranks today must be apprised of the new culture that now invades the classroom. Crossing any of the lines established by bureaucrats or by judicial decisions comprises grounds for teacher discipline and/or dismissal.

New Cultural Paradigm

Teachers must now be aware that some students make up accusations against them, generated in order to run them off, or draw attention to themselves. The number of teachers that have experienced student aggression in person and online is staggering. As often stated, the numbers of these aggressions are woefully underreported.

Another issue is parental acceptance and validation of students' accusations toward teachers. Sometimes parents react violently toward teachers, based solely on the word of their children via text message. A tearful phone call by a student during class may bring a parent storming into a classroom after school. Parents who resort to violence or aggression, in reaction to their children's prompting, are bulldozing their ways across the campuses of public schools. This is shameful and abusive. Are teachers just supposed to accept this abuse? Where are the bureaucrats when things like this occur?

In the Past

Teachers were held in higher esteem in the recent past. This is not the case today. The students are the ones held in high esteem, and they know it. Why has this changed so drastically? One of the reasons is that bureaucrats and the political elite made decisions to implement policies that placed students at the center of education universe, a place traditionally occupied by teachers. Another reason is for political clout with voters—usually Democratic voters.

When students are designated special needs by an IEP, accommodations are then put into place. The accommodations, once stipulated by the adults, must be followed. One of the more frustrating elements for teachers of students with special needs accommodations is often the sole authority of the student to decide when and how work might be accomplished. Not all students have this prerogative. But to those that do, deadlines mean little.

Students can fall back on IEP statements giving them sole discretion to ask for extensions—even after an assignment was introduced months in advance. Simple stress and choices to procrastinate on the parts of students are now the teacher's responsibility to overlook. As a result, acquiescence must occur and accommodations must be adhered to, with respect to the overriding choices of the students.

When a group is weakened by law, they become weak in the eyes of the public. This is where teachers are today and, to reiterate, this is the opposite of where students are today. The following is an example of a conversation this author experienced with a special education director.

> **Dr. Zarra**: Hi Mrs. J. I was wondering whether your student will have completed her project on time?
>
> **Mrs. J.**: Hello, Dr. Z. No, unfortunately not. But you are aware that she has an IEP and can request an extension of any work past any deadline she feels anxious about.
>
> **Dr. Z.**: Yes, I am aware of her modifications. Do the self-initiated extensions also pertain to projects given five months ago? I mean, she has had five months. The project is due in two weeks.
>
> **Mrs. J.**: According to her IEP she has every right to change whatever she needs to, in order to comply with the IEP. She is under stress right now and hasn't started the project.
>
> **Dr. Z.**: Yes, but she still has two weeks before the deadline, and this is why I contacted you in advance.
>
> **Mrs. J.**: The fact that she may have procrastinated is part of her disability. We must comply with the IEP, whether we like it or not. It is the law.
>
> **Dr. Z.**: Oh, we shall comply with the law. But there is nothing in the IEP that stipulates anything other than my having to accept her work on her terms. The grading of the work is up to me. Have a great day.
>
> **Mrs. J.**: Thanks. You are correct about the grading.

These types of incidents are becoming the norm with student modifications. Add the 504 work modifications to the IEP program modifications, and it would not be uncommon for the average middle and secondary public school teachers to have dozens of these modifications spread throughout their classes.

Teachers as Exemplars

Teachers are supposed to be examples, even when they are disrespected, ridiculed, and ripped apart on social media for being those examples. Conversely, students between the ages of sixteen to eighteen are not expected to know better. These are children, after all. So many students commit adult acts all the time, implying that they know exactly what they are doing, except when they are caught. Nevertheless, they are highly protected.

One of the most ridiculous examples of this is an eighteen-year-old student in high school who is treated as school property, subsequently graduates, and heads to college. Such a student is still eighteen, but is not treated as he would have been treated just a few months earlier.

When is an eighteen-year-old not an eighteen-year-old? The answer is when he heads off to college, where students are somehow expected to experiment with adult behaviors more regularly and be applauded for it. College is also the place where parents have little to no say.

LEGAL REMEDIES

Legal remedies surrounding violence against teachers are being discussed nationally. Law schools are digging in deeply on teacher-assault cases. Legislators are beginning to reexamine issues of safety for teachers in public education.[9] However, districts fear lawsuits and bad reputations.

The fear is real that one teacher calling the police, or filing a lawsuit against a district for allowing an unsafe workplace environment, could spell doom for many administrators. If that were to occur, then a tidal wave of lawsuits might follow.[10] One must question why so many of the reports of violence against teachers are covered up, and not reported to the police and the media, as they should be.[11]

Dozens of studies on teacher violence draw many of the same conclusions. The literature also points to the same general conclusion. That is,

> Collectively, educators' perceived threats of violence, as well as lack of support services, classroom behavioral management and stress management training may impact their psychological and professional well-being and performance. Similarly, several researchers found teachers consistently reported a lack of support services and training for preventing and managing school violence. In sum, the research highlights many problematic issues with schools that are associated with high rates of teacher-directed violence.[12]

It has been deemed by the courts (the 7th Circuit specifically), that "a special education teacher cannot sue her school district in Federal Court for injuries suffered while trying to block an autistic child from hitting her with a chair."[13] This is in line with some teacher experiences shared with this author, where states require teachers to implement and maintain hands-off policies, even if they are being assaulted. Deflecting and avoiding is the preference, and not neutralizing the attack, especially an attack from a special needs student.

Many heard the outcry when police restrained an autistic child, after he assaulted a teacher and would not comply with police directions. Many people reacted to seeing an elementary student cuffed at the biceps because his wrists were too small for the restraints. In Okeechobee Achievement Academy, the ten-year-old autistic boy was taken away in handcuffs, as a result of an incident that occurred months earlier.

The boy did not like a certain paraprofessional in his classroom, so he kicked and punched the individual. There were injuries to the paraprofessional, as a result of the assault. There was an arrest warrant out for the boy and, after he returned months later from home study, he was arrested. While being taken away, his mother recorded the incident on her cell phone. The boy was heard saying, "Don't touch me," and "I don't understand why."[14]

A Broken System

These types of incidents only serve to underscore a broken system. Legal remedies fall short. If only incidents like these were anomalies and exceptions. Unfortunately, they are not. Children with special needs are not getting the assistance they need to develop self-control. In turn, they affect their classrooms and take away learning from others when outbursts and incidents occur. It is incidents like these that have teachers fed up.

Should there be zero tolerance for each incident involving special needs students that occurs? What about zero tolerance for regular education students? If one's actions are tolerated, and another's actions are not tolerated, the issues of equity and targeting take on another dimension toward a discussion on equity.

Special needs and special education cases should be handled with one perspective in mind. That is, was there infliction of pain, or injury, upon another person? Whether he or she understands it or not should be largely irrelevant. If the student does not understand what he or she did in assaulting a teacher, then it is only reasonable that the student will not understand the consequences. Therefore, there is no psychological harm in disciplining the student, by removing him or her, in order to protect the teacher and the students in the classroom.

All too often, discipline is merely a temporary removal of a student from his or her environment, and the student is returned to his peers after a short respite. This strategy has serious risk and potential failure written all over it. The risk increases with no serious effort to change behaviors.

In 2009, the Government Accountability Office detailed hundreds of cases of restraining special needs students in schools, including twenty children who died from the restraints. All of these cases involved children with disabilities.[15] Clearly something is wrong with the system of education that does not know what to do with so many special needs children being included in regular classes.

In some cases, there are classroom aides or trained paraprofessionals in classrooms. School psychologists are now assigned to campuses, either dedicated or shared. Yet there are not enough aides or mental health professionals to go around. The system of local law enforcement is trained to enforce laws that apply in ways that state laws allow. But the assaults first have to be reported.

A CHANGE IN PERSPECTIVE

Only more recently, due to increased numbers of assaults, states are referring to assault as criminal, which then involves the police. On a personal level, police have been summoned to local school districts on several occasions, as a result of students assaulting either teachers or their fellow students—including a recent case where an emotionally disturbed high school student brought a knife in his backpack.

Violent special needs students' actions have become so common that federal courts send such cases to state and local courts. In some cases, student's violent actions in classrooms became so commonplace that teachers and principals stop documenting behaviors. Sometimes situations turn very bad and people die.[16]

These are reasons why bureaucrats and educators must take hard looks at their policies of inclusion, while at the same time, legislators and law enforcement officials must examine different methods of dealing with special needs students who act out. This should be true for any student that causes violence in schools, whether public, charter, alternative, or private.

PARENTAL POWER

Parents seem much more inclined to forego decorum and protocols when it comes to their children. In decades past, parents were content to hover over their children. They have acted as helicopters for several years. Now they act more like bulldozers, plowing forward to achieve their will on behalf of their children. The obvious but sometimes misplaced point here is that children first learn both respect and disrespect from home.[17]

Challenging the teacher, rather than working alongside the teacher, seems more the status quo for parents of today's Generation Z students. There is a very real shift that has occurred in the culture, when it comes to the structure of authority in schools and homes. Teachers are doubted and their veracity is challenged regularly. The effort of the teacher even to protect against being assaulted is questioned if the teacher steps in to protect other students from harm—and that alone should speak volumes.

When a student assaults a teacher, school psychologists and others wonder what the teacher did to trigger the assault. Present also in the speculation are parents. They question the environment and whether there are enough parental-type positive statements and love and nurture being communicated by the teacher to the student.

It is not enough that a teacher is injured. Efforts to *dethrone* students from their centrist position in the education universe are often met with disdain. The aspersions that descend upon the teachers' actions and judgment become reasons for their own assaults. What more can be expected from bureaucratic power flipping, where the teacher is at risk of becoming a casualty of the power of the students and their parents?

A certain level of power brings respect, when used properly. Without personal accountability there is often great difficulty in finding balance. In many ways, public education is very much out of balance. We can thank the bureaucrats and politicians for a substantial amount of this imbalance.

FEAR OF ACTION

Politicians and bureaucrats are reluctant to call for arrests of students who act out violently, and are more inclined to make excuses for their behaviors. This disinclination results in passing laws to support their decisions to overlook student behaviors. Anything to the contrary would affect some of their constituent groups' political support.

In some states, the teachers' unions are some of the largest supporters of politicians. However, racial and ethnic civil rights groups also tend toward one political party, which sets up some conflicts of interest for politicians. Any policy that supports teachers, yet involves increases of discipline of protected groups, places constituents at odds with each other. How is this good for either side? This cannot be good for students.

A litigious society is highly restrictive—even in the face of doing what is right. Most school psychologists and intervention strategy experts are in the same camp. Combining the two means school personnel are cautioned to take care to understand there is always something triggering or driving students to act in the extreme. The message is to avoid lawsuits at *all cost*.

So, in efforts to reclassify student behaviors, behavioral psychologists inform a new generation of teachers that human behavior is *caused*. The student himself, or herself, is not completely to blame. Ironically, someone or something else is to be blamed, illustrating that the student may be a victim of his or her own positioning as center of the education universe.[18]

Inexperience Speaks Volumes

One criticism levied upon school psychologists is their limited time spent in the classroom. Education professionals that spent significant time in the classroom trenches before rising in their specialty careers are much more respected by teachers. Lacking significant classroom time means that working directly with students in emerging generations also is lacking.

Today's students are very different than those of a decade ago. However, in their defense, psychologists, like others with caseloads at schools, are so overburdened and snowed under with paperwork, that they do not always have the time to spend in classrooms, to observe the problems for which they offer solutions. If teachers used these reasons for not managing their classrooms, they would be evaluated poorly. Many teachers are overwhelmed with programs and drowning in assessments, yet each teacher is expected to accomplish daily miracles.

The uniqueness of schools sometimes means that disciplinary measures are handled differently, even with the same distributive disciplinary policy in hand. For example, finding "reasons" as to why a student hits a teacher in the nose with his or her fist is very important. Sometimes incidents such as these are considered accidental, or part of the expectations when working with students who may be emotionally or mentally disturbed.

Severely disabled students can sometimes be very violent, but there is always the question as to whether they understand any of their actions. Sometimes a student is just mean-spirited and decides to act on his or her natural inclination at the moment, special needs or not. Certainly, cases like these are unique and should be handled as such.

In the main, exploring students' reasons for actions should not be of primary concern, if consequences are not equally explored. The issue is, what are the consequences, so that the student can learn from the error in judgment, or error in action? Without correction, how long might it be before one such student grows up and is held accountable for something much more deeply contrived, or expressed?[19]

Ask any group of veteran teachers of a decade or more experience, and they can usually refer back in time to former students who they identified as exhibiting certain precursors toward serious future violent actions. Today, the numbers of flagrant actions and assaults by students are greater in number, and it makes no difference the student's race or background.

Teachers in lower grades are experiencing the precursors first hand. Some of the stories from elementary schools are frightening. Yet teachers are expected to work with these students, putting themselves at greater risk in the process.

Teachers are expected to perform wonders in the face of less respect from parents and students, and lessened support from administrators. Take for example one of the many risk factors for teachers today: the *bipolar student*. This student "can experience great irritability, building to a rage if not recognized and dealt with in an appropriate and timely manner."[20] Managing students such as these is way above the pay grade of the average teacher.

TAKING A STAND

Certainly, standing up for education equity means standing up for families—all families, even those with mainstreamed special needs students who might very well be on the receiving end of the violence from one of their very own. However, the model and the methods are not, and should never be, a one-size-fits-all paradigm.

Challenging this conclusion might best be viewed through the lens of two overarching questions. The first question is related to Common Core, and it asks: *Have Common Core's advanced rigors added to, or diminished, academic and emotional frustrations of students, including special needs students?*

The time has come for education professionals, bureaucrats, legislators, social-service professionals, psychologists, politicians, and classroom teachers to sit down and talk. Part of their conversations must address the second question: *Are special needs students truly being served in our public schools, or do they need schools that specifically focus on their styles of learning, and understand their disabilities professionally and practically?*

SOCIOCULTURAL CHANGES IMPACT SCHOOLS AND STUDENTS

States under ESSA are taking advantage of advancing their more localized education and adopting new curriculum and standards. In some cases, these new adoptions have incorporated cultural changes and schools will expect these changes to be part of classroom decorum, going forward.

For example, a recent political impact is the latest revision to *California's History-Social Science Curriculum Framework and State Standards*. The changes represent examples of interest groups affecting bureaucrats. California will now include in new social studies textbooks and curricula what some consider important historical contributions of those outside the mainstream of sexual identity and expression. Certain groups, often marginalized by society in the past, are now incorporated into certain states' curriculum, while others are left out.

Teachers that hold to the views of traditional marriage are now instructed not to assume students abide by the traditional model of marriage and that it is offensive to some to speak of a mother and a father, or refer to students by male and female.

Teachers, not only in America, are coming under scrutiny for not recognizing a student's personal claim of gender and sexuality, including references to genderless parents.[21] Can these actions be considered an assault on traditional American culture and upon teachers and families wishing to discuss the merits of a nuclear family, but who must now exercise caution not to refer to genders and traditional relationships?[22]

Bureaucracy is handcuffing teachers of previous generations. Unlike the cuffing of violent ten-year-olds, this cuffing is figurative and politically expedient. Sociocultural changes do impact our schools and classrooms.

More often than not, the Supreme Court must get involved, which can lead to even greater concerns,[23] depending on the political complexion of the court. Yes, sociocultural changes impact schools and students, as well as teachers.

POLICY BASED ON RACE?

Lawsuits have been brought by the ACLU and other groups, such as the Dolores Huerta Foundation, which sued on behalf of the growing number of minority students being suspended or expelled. The accusations brought in the lawsuits are that districts and administrators, because of policies, are basically targeting certain groups of students for suspension and expulsion. Among these groups are especially higher percentages of black and Hispanic students.[24]

Having to Think Twice

Given today's student disciplinary considerations, the students' actions are no longer enough to be considered for immediate heavy disciplinary measures. In many states, the reasons for permissible suspension and expulsion have been slimmed down drastically. Before administrators can suspend a student, or before a board can recommendation an expulsion, questions must be asked as to whether the school or district provided various and additional opportunities to keep the students in school. They must ask themselves quietly, "Will we be sued because of the removal of a student in a protected class?"

On campus intervention and *re-immersion* programs are established, so as to keep assailants on campus. Even in the most chronic of cases, these extra pressures are applied. The new reality is that discipline of anyone black or Hispanic may now be subject to questioning, or even ACLU litigation, and linked to targeting or profiling allegations. Where does this leave teachers when the majority of their students are from one or both of these demographics?

When a teacher has to consider a student's race or ethnicity before sending the student to the office, or when a principal thinks about the same thing before suspending a student, risk levels increase. Teachers must check themselves to see if they are subconsciously viewing race as an issue, in meting out disciplinary referrals.

Teachers must query their motivation to see if there is some underlying, subconscious racial bias toward a student, or a student that is part of a group, before removing a student. National data indicate that teacher's hands are becoming increasingly more tied, forcing them to think twice, fearful of bureaucracy and lawsuits. Take for example, the state of Delaware.

In Delaware, recent legislation not only sought to limit the reasons students can be disciplined, but attempted to "address troubling disparities regarding race, disabilities, and gender. African-American students made up 32 percent of the student body in 2013, but accounted for 62 percent of out-of-school suspensions. Students with disabilities also made up 13 percent of the student body, but accounted for 24 percent of out-of-school suspensions, according to data from the Delaware Department of Education."[25]

The underlying motivation for the legislation is that there is not enough done to understand the internal conflicts of certain groups, "including students of color, the emotionally disturbed, and students with learning disorders that cause the outbursts and unruliness of some students."[26] The reader should be curious to determine whether a metric exists whereby bureaucrats could measure when enough had been done.

Teachers and administrators in many states must now take part in required *culture-shaping intervention training* that considers the comprehensive cultural and racial backgrounds of students. Progress is being made to reprogram teachers toward being more sensitive to those in protected classes. This training is becoming the latest mandate for some school districts. The prediction is that soon, the training may become required by some states, embedded in their teacher credential programs.

Modern administrators share the responsibility of understanding reasons for students' words or actions, especially those from a protected class. Anytime a student, regardless of demographic, is kept in a classroom after expressing violent behaviors, the system appears to favor the student over the safety of the teacher and the other students in the classroom. Administrations must learn to balance this. Social justice victories, over and against safety, are not victories for all.

COMMON SENSE

Certainly, any teacher or school that has policies or practices that treat students unfairly should be called out. This is common sense. Equity should slice both ways, and not favor one group over others. Questioning every teacher's motives or each school's policies of discipline because of a few students who either complain about unfair treatment or actually experience this unfairness is an overreach. Yet this is our nation's current posture and teachers must either deal with it or lobby with their associations and politicians for change.

Most understand that where a larger percentage of minority students attend school, the chances that more minority referrals will be submitted are higher. That is not targeting. That is just mathematics. That being said, due to the hyper-attention being paid to issues of race today, even the mathematics is subject to civil rights' accusations of profiling. For the most part, it is schools where students of color are in the minority numerically that elicit most of the concerns.

Bureaucrats need to spend time in schools to understand the reasons for student outbursts and violent behaviors. Most are completely out of touch with the realities that exist in today's public schools. They listen to lobbyists and constituent groups forced to comply with legal decisions, rather than to research and draw conclusions for themselves. Student discipline has now become politicized, and it began in earnest most recently under the Obama Administration.

GAINING THE ATTENTION OF THE BUREAUCRACY

Bureaucracy is a term describing governmental structures and decision-making processes. These structures and pressures comprise the vast majority of decisions made in the bureaucratic chain of authority. Whether state or federal government, public or private education, the politics of bureaucracies can be somewhat contentious. In terms of public education, teachers are pressured from many sides. The irony is that teachers fighting bureaucracies often join another bureaucracy to continue the fight.

Most teachers are unwilling to take part in ideological fights. They just want to do their jobs. Sometimes teachers become marginalized over issues, pressed into taking sides over one or more types of social or political agenda. Other times, there is general consensus among teachers of all political stripes and ideologies. There is no better place to demonstrate this unity than with leading efforts to actively lobby for safer working environments for educators.

These kinds of efforts gain the attention of federal, state, and local governments. However, when teachers depart from what unifies them, they come under assaults of a different kind. Sometimes these assaults come from within their own ranks, which is another issue unto itself. For some reason, many who examine public school teachers seem to conclude that most teachers are tolerant of most everything in culture. The fact is that nearly all teachers, whether members of a political party or not, are quite intolerant of extreme intolerance.

Extreme Intolerance

Extreme intolerance is occurring toward those standing for traditional American values, including marriage and the family. The same can be found for teachers espousing evangelical Christian lifestyles, or Muslim culture. Most recently, any teacher voting for Donald Trump was marginalized by teacher associations. Others expressed dislike and hatred, some with revolting actions and personal denunciations.

Bureaucrats, social activists, and some in the media are found labeling groups that support a moral cause different from their own as "hate groups." They may also find themselves on the receiving end of death threats, ostracism, and lawsuits. For better or for worse, decisions made at the top of many state governments impact all, and some decisive actions will not make everyone happy. Bureaucracies that directly impact education need to be held in check by teachers. This is the only way teachers will be able to muster greater protections and further their careers in the classrooms across the United States.

IMPACTS OF SCHOOL BOARDS

The last thing that school boards and elected local bureaucrats want is to hear reports of violence at the schools they represent. Violence involving students with special needs or in special education programs is a close second to hearing of increased suspensions of students of color. School boards are often representative of community demographics. Sometimes they are out of the loop of occurrences of violence on school campuses. Other times they first hear about violence from media reports.

Reports of Violence

Media reports of violence in schools, for any reason, are poor publicity and add fear to those attending a school. Teachers and students know those students that are more prone toward outbursts and have tendencies to lash out physically. Once an incident is reported, sometimes the school bureaucracy swallows the report. The fact is, a school with a record of violence must also have a record of referrals, suspensions, or expulsions. If it does not, something is very wrong.

Under the guise of privacy and personnel issues, schools can protect the privacy of the student and the teacher. In all candor, not everyone hides their feelings regarding teacher assaults—especially if it happens to them, or someone they care about.

Violence Minimized

An example of this is the Rolling Hills Elementary School of the Huntsville, Alabama School District. Referring to a report of students assaulting teachers at the elementary level, Interim Superintendent Tom Drake called such reports by the media "fake news." He stated in December 2016 that what teachers are experiencing and are reporting as injuries is "nothing out of the ordinary,"[27] and implied that the media is playing up the issues larger than reality.

Drake added that the younger students are really not guilty of assault. He stated, "Words like assault, violence, that's inflammatory and often obscure the fact that we're talking about babies."[28] Drake had drawn the conclusion that so many administrators and bureaucrats have drawn. That is, the age and size of the elementary students make it untenable that a true definition of assault is satisfied when there is an injury caused by a younger student.

Fast-forward to May 2017. One teacher claimed it was a slap in the face to make the claim that reports of assaults were fake news. The teacher contended adamantly, "It's a dangerous place to go to work."[29] After having been shown photos of teachers' injuries, as well as finding items such as knives and bullets outside classroom doors, the Huntsville City School Board President, Elisa Ferrell, was presented with the evidence. One of the responses from Ferrell was shocking, in that she stated, "If this is happening in the classroom, then they should be more actively engaging in getting the district's attention."[30]

Teachers in the district said they repeatedly tried to get the district's attention. The interim superintendent only minimized the assaults as "accidents," and justified them as students who may "come up and hug your leg, but might also kick you in the shin." One district teacher was bold enough to counter the board president and the interim superintendent by adding, "These are not accidents when a child comes up to you and hits you as hard as they can. It's not an accident when a child throws a chair at you."[31] Another teacher added, "I don't understand how these are accidents. They mean to hurt you."[32] Yet another teacher stated, "I think we have an administration whose hands are tied."[33]

Just Moving On

Why is it that teachers are not reporting more violent acts against them? Drake's responses to the reports of assault against teachers in Huntsville are a good indication why teachers just take the injury and move on. They just sort of grimace and come to expect that being injured by students must be part of the job description.

Teachers are also fearful of retaliation if they complain, which is exactly what some of the injured teachers expressed to the Occupational Safety and Health Administration.[34] This being the case, it is likely that such a precedent is found amongst many teachers in public schools. This means, then, that crimes and assaults against teachers are woefully underreported, because of the fear of reprisal.[35] Teachers just put it behind them and move on.

Bureaucracy and politics may be inseparable from American education. Even as American teachers generally comply and support bureaucrats who form education policy, they also fear that the loss of their authority will continue to lead to more violence against them in their classrooms. Bureaucrats, then, should bear some of the blame for the increased violence. Citizens who care about public education should step up and hold their leaders accountable.

REVERSING THE TREND

There can be little doubt as to the impact of state and federal bureaucrats and politicians on the matter of teacher attrition. There are some things these leaders can do to slow the exodus of teachers from schools. But it will take some compromise and serious work to reverse the trend. Bureaucracy is a blanket that covers much of education. From curriculum to discipline policy, teachers are told what to do by those wielding power at various levels.

Bureaucrats are not making matters easier for teachers. Each passing year seems to bring more constraints upon teachers, and less upon students' behaviors. Protections are added for students and those who happen to win legal actions, or lobby their state houses effectively. Consequently, all of these things affect students and families. When a group wins and attention is drawn to the victors as they attend schools, it usually means another group has to sacrifice their time.

Parents must insist on some things from bureaucrats, on behalf of their children. Teachers must continue to speak on behalf of themselves and their students. Both should insist on safe schools, a challenging learning environment, and policies that favor academics over social issues.

The focus on social justice and restorative programs are causing very serious unintended consequences, which are not helping to alleviate the teacher exodus. For one thing, bureaucrats did not ask teachers or parents whether focusing on such programs would add or detract from the education of all students. Removing personal accountability from students and placing it squarely onto teachers is a reversal of the wrong kind.

Bureaucrats should be held accountable for not holding students accountable. When human problems occur because of policy decisions that affect those in the trenches, the leaders must hear about these problems. In other words, to reiterate, bureaucrats should be held accountable for not holding students accountable.

If teachers were to sense support for their concerns from their local school boards, they would be less inclined to exit the profession. In fact, they would probably be emboldened to work harder and make the best of their situations.

Conversely, there is no denying the facts that teachers are being assaulted in larger numbers than ever before. What are the plans of politicians to reverse this trend? One cannot be about reversing the trend of teachers leaving the profession without first paying attention to solving what may be a major cause for the attrition.

Teachers have the professional responsibility to stand alongside colleagues who have been threatened by students. If this occurs on campus, on-site administrators should send the strongest possible message that violence at their schools will not be tolerated and will be dealt with swiftly. Then they must deal with it or be held accountable by local education stakeholders and community members. Once bureaucratic snafus occur between PBIS strategists and administrators—and they will occur—it is incumbent upon the administrators to support their teachers. If they do not, teachers may leave their schools, or leave the profession altogether.

Any student assaulting a teacher should not be in attendance at school for a very, very long time. A student assailant should not be able to return to the school at which the assault occurred. Parents should see to it that this is the case. Furthermore, school boards are expected to protect their teachers. If this protection breaks down, then teachers must be willing to stand up and refuse to work in a dangerous environment.

Student assailants must receive counseling and, of course, so should the injured teachers. School districts must develop action plans to keep teachers safe, and these plans must be tied to accreditation by the state. Elections have consequences, and elected officials need to be reminded of this truism. Only in this way can bureaucrats and politicians be held accountable to the very system they helped to create.

Parents must insist on safe schools for their children. They must rise up and take measures to express their concerns—even if it means going to the local media. Every effort should be made to convince bureaucrats and politicians that schools must be safe for children and that teachers must also feel safe at work.

Retaining teachers in public school classrooms should be a priority for states. When teachers leave, a little bit of the soul of the next generation is chipped away. State courts must begin to exercise common sense with law and policy, when making decisions in cases. What is best for all children should be the standard. Only then can we ever hope to realize true education for students in this nation.

NOTES

1. Brenda Isaacs. "High school district policy raises questions." *The Bakersfield Californian*. November 21, 2017, p. 21.
2. Jane Meredith Adams. "Most teachers in California say they need more training in alternatives to suspensions, survey says." *EdSource*. May 7, 2017. Retrieved from https://edsource.org/2017/most-teachers-in-california-say-they-need-more-training-in-alternatives-to-suspensions-survey-finds/581195.
3. Ibid.
4. Ibid.
5. Ibid.
6. Ernest J. Zarra, III. *Helping parents understand the minds and hearts of Generation Z*. Lanham, MD: Rowman & Littlefield, 2017.
7. New York State United Teachers. "Safe schools against violence in education act (project SAVE)." January 2001. Retrieved from https://www.nysut.org/~/media/files/nysut/resources/2001/february/ib_healthandsafety_ll_ssav.pdf?la=en.
8. Ibid.
9. Perris E. Nelson. "Student-on-teacher violence: A proposed solution." June 2016. *Brigham Young University Education and Law Journal* 2016, no. 2. Article 4. Retrieved from http://digitalcommons.law.byu.edu/cgi/viewcontent.cgi?article=1389&context=elj.
10. Edward F. Dragan. "School liability and negligent supervision of children with disabilities." *Education Expert*. January 16, 2014. Retrieved from http://education-expert.com/2014/01/school-liability-reasonable-supervision-children-disabilities/.
11. Scottie Hughes. "Why is violence against teachers being covered up?" *Townhall*. October 7, 2013. Retrieved from https://townhall.com/columnists/scottiehughes/2013/10/07/why-is-violence-against-teachers-being-covered-up-n1718394.
12. Linda A Reddy, Dorothy L. Espelage, Susan D. McMahon, et al. "Violence against teachers: Case studies from the APA task force." December 4, 2013. *International Journal of School & Educational Psychology* 1, no. 4, pp. 231–245 (viz. p. 243). Retrieved from http://www.tandfonline.com/doi/full/10.1080/21683603.2013.837019. See also Dorothy L. Espelage, Mrinalini A. Rao, and Rhonda G. Craven. "Theories of cyberbullying." In *Principles of cyberbullying research: Definitions, measures, and methodology*, Sherrie Bauman, Donna Cross, and Jenny Walker (Eds.). 2013. New York, New York: Routledge, pp. 49–67. Ernest J. Zarra, III. *Teacher-student relationships: Crossing into the emotional, physical, and sexual realms*. Lanham, MD: Rowman & Littlefield, 2013, see pp. 99–123.
13. Staff. "7th Circuit holds school not constitutionally liable for autistic student's violent assaults." *Handle with care*. December 2012. Retrieved from http://handlewithcare.com/7th-circuit-holds-school-not-constitutionally-liable-for-autistic-students-violent-assaults.
14. Jacqueline Howard. "10-year-old boy with autism arrested at school." *CNN*. April 24, 2017. Retrieved from http://www.cnn.com/2017/04/21/health/autism-florida-10-year-old-arrested-bn/index.html.
15. Lester Holt. "Boy cries in pain after being handcuffed at school." *NBC Nightly News*. August 4, 2017. Retrieved from https://www.nbcnews.com/nightly-news/video/boy-cries-in-pain-after-being-handcuffed-at-school-498517059817.
16. Evie Blad. "Student, teacher shot dead in California special needs classroom." *Education Week*. April 10, 2017. Retrieved from http://blogs.edweek.org/edweek/rulesforengage

ment/2017/04/san_bernardino_school_shooting_a_possible_murder-suicide_police_say.html.

17. Zarra. *Helping parents understand the minds and hearts of Generation Z.*

18. Peter Tait. "Causes of growing mental health problems sit largely within schools." *The Telegraph.* December 2, 2015. Retrieved from http://www.telegraph.co.uk/education/educationopinion/12025711/Schools-largely-to-blame-for-rising-mental-health-issues.html. See also Nancy Colier. "What to do about the people who blame you for everything." *Psychology Today.* December 13, 2015. Retrieved from https://www.psychologytoday.com/blog/inviting-monkey-tea/201512/what-do-about-the-people-who-blame-you-everything.

19. Derek Hawkins. "Oregon man carries mother's severed head into a grocery store, stabs a clerk." May 16, 2017. *The Washington Post.* Retrieved from https://www.washingtonpost.com/news/morning-mix/wp/2017/05/16/oregon-man-carries-mothers-severed-head-into-a-grocery-then-stabs-a-clerk-police-say/?utm_term=.583e07c69aea. See also George Houde. "Man who beheaded mom in 2003 gets transfer from Elgin mental hospital." *Chicago Tribune.* October 13, 2017. Retrieved from http://www.chicagotribune.com/suburbs/elgin-courier-news/news/ct-man-killed-mother-seeks-elgin-release-met-20160204-story.html.

20. Staff. "Symptoms and accommodations." *Juvenile Bipolar Research Foundation.* n.d. Retrieved from https://www.jbrf.org/page-for-families/educational-issues-facing-children-with-bipolar-disorder/symptoms-and-accomodations/.

21. Martha Azzi and Nelson Groom. "Schools banned from using the terms 'mum and dad' and boys told to dress up as girls in 'non-gender-specific free play.'" *Daily Mail Australia.* July 20, 2016. Retrieved from http://www.dailymail.co.uk/news/article-3699679/Schools-banned-using-terms-mum-dad-boys-told-dress-girls-non-gender-specific-free-play.html. See also Staff. "He? She? Ze? Colleges add gender-free pronouns for students." *CBS News.* September 18, 2015. Retrieved from https://www.cbsnews.com/news/harvard-university-colleges-gender-free-pronouns-transgender-genderqueer-students/.

22. Ryan Dailey. "Teacher requests students use gender-neutral pronouns: Parents divided." *USA Today.* September 20, 2017. Retrieved from https://www.usatoday.com/story/news/nation-now/2017/09/20/teacher-requests-students-use-gender-neutral-pronouns/687647001/. See also Todd Starnes. "NC school to teachers: Don't call students 'boys and girls.'" *Fox News.* August 16, 2016. Retrieved from http://www.foxnews.com/opinion/2016/08/16/nc-school-to-teachers-dont-call-students-boys-and-girls.html.

23. Kate Shellnutt. "Christian orgs labeled hate groups on top charity site." *Christianity Today.* August 24, 2017. Retrieved from http://www.christianitytoday.com/news/2017/june/christian-charities-labeled-hate-groups-guidestar-splc-frc.html.

24. Ibid.

25. Jessica Masulli Reyes and Matthew Albright. "Bill aims to cut number of out-of-school suspensions." *The News Journal.* May 6, 2016. Retrieved from http://www.delawareonline.com/story/news/education/2016/05/06/bill-aims-cut-number-out--school-suspensions/83723788/0.

26. Ibid.

27. Paul Dughi. "School district says reports on teachers are 'fake news.'" *WAAY-TV Report.* December 16, 2016. Retrieved from https://medium.com/@pauldughi/school-district-says-reports-of-assaults-on-teachers-are-fake-news-c90bef170830.

28. Ibid.

29. Heather Mathis. "Rolling Hills Elementary teachers show evidence of classroom violence." *WAAY-TV Report.* May 19, 2017. Retrieved from http://www.waaytv.com/story/35470691/rolling-hills-elementary-teachers-show-evidence-of-classroom-violence.

30. Ibid.

31. Ibid.

32. Ibid.

33. Ibid.

34. Dughi. "School district says reports on teachers are 'fake news.'"

35. Ibid.

Chapter Three

Teachers Fighting for Change

> The death of the classroom teacher may have been greatly exaggerated, but their role is going to change, according to the head of the one of the largest international education groups. Technology has long been seen as undermining the traditional teacher's role.... Technology is both helping transform the way children learn and threatening to make teachers obsolete. For some, this is a welcome development. It may even solve one of our most intractable problems, in making the teacher recruitment crisis go away. But if the skills and knowledge that a teacher traditionally imparts are available elsewhere, does that mean teachers will soon be obsolete?[1]

Education in America is becoming more and more marginalized along political and social lines. Money is being poured into the American public education system, which is keeping it afloat. Aside from the financial elements, there has been so much debate over school accountability and teacher accountability, yet very little discussion about student accountability. This is an imbalance caused by bureaucrats' politically fearful fingers tipping the scale of equity. Students sense this, and they have a deeply ingrained sense of entitlement. Most of what teachers sense is their own inequality.

If a third grade student, while on a field trip to a zoo, loses control of his temper and injures or kills an animal, he or she will be arrested and fines will be levied. Why then should students be treated any differently when they hurt a teacher, or another student, because of an expression of similar violence?

Why should an animal in a public zoo be more protected than teachers in public schools? Why is tolerance of violence considered in one place and not considered in another? In all candor, if a principal of a school campus or a parent was directly assaulted, it would only be common sense that these situations would be handled very differently.

THE MARGINALIZATION OF EDUCATION

Teacher education programs in colleges and universities include a course here and there on exceptional children, or special education. However, unlike specially trained special needs teachers, most classroom teachers are not equipped to have special needs students in their classrooms.

As a remedy to this shortcoming, teacher education programs should present data and emphasize to their program candidates that there is an increase of violence against teachers coming from special needs and special-education-designated students. Teacher education candidates should also hear that this violence begins as early as transitional kindergarten.

The numbers of teachers punched, slapped, kicked, and verbally abused by children today are way up. Teacher candidates should also challenge the expectations they assume when they are hired. As it stands, teacher education presents marginal material, in terms of teacher readiness. In terms of education, teachers are marginalized as well.

Teachers Are Marginal

Teachers are told to handle their own classroom discipline. As a result, injuries occur that teachers simply learn to "live with." Teachers want to be known as classroom-trained content experts, yet do not care to possess the title that comes with the inability to handle their own classroom discipline.

The fact is that teachers have very few tools at their disposal to handle major classroom disruptions. If a teacher punishes a student, his or her feelings get hurt. They are quick to inform their parents that their teacher is mean. Parents want to know what is wrong with the teacher for treating their child this way, or that way. To illustrate, if a recess is missed, the teacher's actions are called into question. Since all students need playtime, some parents and administrators think it is unconscionable for teachers to withhold playtime as punishment for not obeying in class.

If a field trip is scheduled and certain students would be more of a liability than others, these students are allowed to go, since a field trip is not a classroom event and is extracurricular. A principal's policy can marginalize teachers by circumventing classroom or even school policy. Marginal student behavior enables an entitlement mentality for a student, when he or she is not held to the same standard as other students.

The worst part about students who move from *troublesome* to *violent* is that usually within one day, or less, they are placed back into their classes to enjoy *new beginnings* and *fresh starts*. Success is marginal, at best. There always seem to be additional chances for some students, making it seemingly unfair for other students who see these outcomes.

TEACHERS EXITING THE CLASSROOM

Teachers leave the profession for just a few major reasons. One of these major reasons, as addressed earlier, is fear of injury. Teachers that sense an imminent outburst of violence by a student often do their best to take precautions for themselves and their students. They are often concerned about the long-term psychological damage of experiencing violence in a place supposedly set up to protect and nurture. Furthermore, teachers often struggle with their inability to ensure this protection.

Managing a classroom today means managing levels of behaviors and anticipated behaviors earmarked for violence. Regardless of the intervention, some students are *just off*. There must be a set of clear consequences for students that cross the line. Policies without consequences frustrate teachers.

Exposure to Violence

If parents and teachers are at all concerned about the exposure to virtual reality and online game violence, then what about the possibility and reality of actual violence and the effects it has over the long term? What is this type of exposure doing to children? The reality is that a student injuring a teacher, or a person of authority, can have traumatic effects on others and negatively affect the development of all students.

What is the plausibility that the brains of some students experience the emotions attached to *real* violence, when they experience violence through augmented reality and virtual reality games? Teachers battle many elements that enter the classroom and challenge the learning environment. Brains excited by violence are one of these challenges.

How Much Violence Should Be Tolerated?

How much violence should a teacher tolerate in his or her regular classroom? The same should be asked of teachers of special education, or those working with special needs students. At what point is the "had enough" moment reached, to motivate teachers to walk away from their classrooms?

Recently, the "National Center for Education Statistics survey found two-thirds of the approximately 238,000 teachers who left the profession after the 2011–12 school year did so for non-retirement reasons."[2] Teachers are leaving cities like San Francisco, despite efforts to attract and retain them. Other cities, such as Harrisburg, Pennsylvania, are experiencing mass resignations due to violence against teachers.[3]

The same phenomenon occurred recently in Baltimore County public schools. One of the major reasons given is that "every year, hundreds of Baltimore City teachers are injured at work by violent or unruly students, and many school employees believe such incidents have become more common in recent years as a result of the policies aimed at keeping troublesome students in class rather than suspending them."[4]

Economics Brings Choices

Another reason communities see large-scale resignations is economic. As mentioned in an earlier chapter, for some teachers violence is not the primary reason for leaving the classroom. For example, in California, a recent plea was made to bureaucrats. This plea was made on behalf of teachers who could not afford to live in the communities in which they were employed. Apparently, a good number of teachers claimed their salaries and living accommodations made it impossible to work in cities like Los Angeles and San Francisco. In the latter, the city was using the inordinate number of teachers who have left the profession to advance the cause of low-income rentals for San Francisco teachers.

There is no doubt that housing is a factor for teachers leaving a teaching career, in some very expensive cities.[5] However, housing is not at the top of the list of reasons for a mass exodus of public school teachers nationally. Teachers are leaving the profession more often due to violence and other issues behind the scenes.

In terms of the latter, teachers endure behind-the-scenes threats and bullying of parents and students. At the secondary level, there is pressure from administrators to increase graduation rates. Teachers work in compromising environments where grades are sometimes actually tampered with,[6] and this is highly unethical.

Teacher Shaming

Another behind-the-scenes issue is teacher shaming. Teachers who seek to hold the line of school or classroom policies are sometimes called out and shamed. There is no better example of this than the pressure placed on teachers to increase graduation rates, particularly for groups that have been under strict scrutiny by political administrations. A recent conversation yielded this reality, as teachers have been instructed not to fail students of color.

An African-American principal of a local secondary school warned all of his teachers to evaluate blacks and Hispanics with different criteria, so that graduation rates did not decline. In his words, "These kids are not going to college, so do something to get them through." This is terrible, and it is probably more commonplace in American cities than the public is aware. Such a practice is highly unethical.

Once NCLB and high-stakes achievement tests were replaced by Common Core, a reduction in accountability occurred. One of the only measures remaining to evaluate schools is graduation rates. For many teachers, graduation has become another high-stakes assessment, which is highly personalized as a mission. Now race-based grading criteria seems like it is being added to the mix, and teachers are finding a large measure of objectivity is now missing from the package of grading and evaluating students.

Compromise

Another behind-the-scenes pressure placed on teachers is the always-present, conscious effort paid to the reduction of suspensions and expulsions. Principals call out teachers with classes that contain students of color that are failing. There is an unwritten rule of unacceptability today in public schools. That is, students must pass and graduate. Even with no law, teachers are called into the offices of the administrators and are told to find ways.

Teachers also must often compromise their values and convictions to pass verbally defiant and violent students, regardless of the demographic involved. They do so knowing that in the past, current student behaviors would have resulted in immediate suspensions or expulsions. Does anyone still wonder that numbers of assaults are up, but the numbers of these assaults resulting in suspensions and expulsions is down?[7]

There should always be concern as to what is going on in schools in regard to literacy rates, mathematics and reading scores, and high school graduation. However, where is the concern about violence? Regardless of one's background, race, or anything else, it appears that assaults and abuse of teachers are becoming rites of passage along the way to receiving a diploma.

Political Pressure Affecting Teachers

Adding to the frustration in education are the political pressures of some state departments. Politically motivated banning of state businesses because of state disagreements helps no one. States that ban travel to other states because of disagreement with intra-state policies do little to encourage teachers from out of state to move and take up residency in states with opposing viewpoints.

These states may be experiencing teacher shortages because of refusals to recruit teachers from states with different political agendas on social issues, usually pertaining to factions. Whether it is the views of one side or another, or the political decisions made to emphasize disagreement, it all hurts students in the long run. States have only themselves to blame if they cannot fill their classrooms with qualified and well-trained teachers.

For example, a progressive state like California and a more traditional state like Texas are both experiencing shortages in teachers. On the one hand, California bans state employees from traveling to Texas, yet many businesses are fleeing California's high taxes and progressivism for states like Texas.[8]

It would probably not be a stretch to think that traditional teachers from Texas would not feel welcome in California's major city classrooms. This type of political battle does not place children and families first,[9] and certainly does little to attract excellent teachers from around the nation. All of this only adds to the marginalization initiated by politicians. Again, students are the ones who pay the ultimate price.

STATES MAKING CHANGES TO SUPPORT TEACHERS

Change for the sake of change is equivalent to walking backwards on a treadmill and determining that forward progress is being achieved. The perception of movement forward does not necessarily take education anywhere. That being said, some states are actually changing laws and tightening up discipline policies, in order to draw attention to problems of teacher shortages. They are doing so by efforts to protect teachers in classrooms. Here are some examples.

Wisconsin

In Madison, Wisconsin, Madison Teachers Incorporated (MTI) "will institute a civil action against any student who threatens or hits an employee. . . . Typically, the court immediately issues a Temporary Restraining Order (TRO) requiring the student to stay at least 50 feet away from the employee. The TRO is served on the student by a deputy Sheriff."[10]

Three Wisconsin cases have resulted in successes for teachers. These teachers were either threatened and/or assaulted. The actionable threats included:

- "a student (and gang member) who threatened a teacher with the words, 'What if I gun you down?'"[11]
- "a student who kicked and punched a teacher and threatened to kill" the teacher,[12] and
- "a student who yelled at a teacher, 'I going to burn your house down and come to your funeral.'"[13]

Massachusetts

The Massachusetts Teachers Association (MTA) takes advantage of existing criminal statutes to accomplish outcomes similar to as those in Wisconsin. Therefore, when an association member is "threatened or beaten in that state, the attorneys assist the member in filing a criminal complaint against the student."[14]

Attorneys who handle the cases for MTA members have seen numbers of cases tick upward. According to one attorney, Charles Healey, who has handled several of these assault cases, many teachers "have sworn out criminal complaints against parents who have threatened or hit them or disrupted class."[15] Some of Healey's clients expressed discontent and fear and many had reached their breaking point and were "just [so] plain fed-up that they quit their jobs and left teaching soon after being attacked by a student."[16]

Tightening up the policies and protections for teachers is long overdue. Students should never be allowed to cause physical harm to anyone on campus, let alone teachers. On today's school campuses, situations can escalate in a hurry because of the immediacy of technological connectivity.

Many students phone their parents or share with friends immediately at the sign of anything that upsets them. As a result, parents sometimes storm over to their child's school, where verbal altercations occur and assaults sometimes result. Furthermore, students gather and sometimes gang up on a teacher or teacher's aide, as a result of being informed of the upset of one their friends.

MANDATORY EXPULSIONS

Just when there is movement toward regathering our educational wits toward protecting teachers from violent students, other assaults occur. This time parents become the assailants. One such example of an out-of-control parent assaulting a classroom teacher is found in an incident at Alverta B. Gray Schultz Middle School in Hempstead, New York. "Two people, an adult and a juvenile"[17] were arrested after an assault on a teacher inside a Long Island, New York public school.

The arrested parent claimed the classroom teacher placed her hands on her twelve-year-old daughter earlier on the day of the attack. The parent entered campus without security clearance and "waited in the hallway for the teacher."[18] After a brief conversation, the teacher called for security, at which point the parent exploded, shoved the teacher against a wall, and the teacher was "placed in a headlock and thrown to the floor, where she was kicked and punched by several students,"[19] including the assailant's niece.

Both the parent, thirty-four-year-old Annika McKenzie, and her fourteen-year-old niece were arrested for second-degree assault. The parent was also charged with strangulation, since the teacher claimed she was rendered unconscious.[20] Is there any question whether a student involved in such a melee should be expelled?

The state of Michigan passed a law in 1999 that requires "school districts to expel any student grade 6 and above who physically assaults a school employee."[21] This law was challenged and ultimately prevailed when injured teachers showed that the Board failed to live up its requirements under the law, by not enforcing the mandatory expulsion. Recently, the Michigan Supreme Court held that the 1999 law was written and passed so that teachers would be protected "from assault and to assist them in more effectively performing their jobs."[22]

States like Indiana, Pennsylvania, Ohio, and others have set the mark for additional remedies for teachers who experience violence against them. This violence can include statements of threats online via websites, actual physical harm, or verbal threats.

In many cases, Workers' Compensation is available for damages and injuries, medical expenses, and even lost pay. However, Workers' Compensation laws "preclude employees from suing their employers. But employees can sue the student and his parents,"[23] as the following examples illustrate:

- The Indiana State Teachers Association funded a lawsuit by three teachers targeted by a student's Internet website with the moniker "tyme-2-dye." The teachers won $5,000 each.
- Pennsylvania teacher Kathleen Fulmer received $500,000 from a student and his parents for a website that asked for donations for a hitman to help kill the teacher. The student posted doctored images of Fulmer's decapitated body.
- An Ohio court allowed parents to be sued by a teacher who was horribly assaulted by an autistic child, because the parents were aware of the child's violent tendencies and did not warn the teacher.

In order for violence against teachers to garner the attention it needs, it is possible the time has come to allow lawsuits to be brought against school administrators and school districts. Allowing known dangerous and hostile actors access to classrooms where assaults may occur, and creating a hostile workplace in the process, is intolerable. Doing nothing about such conditions should be illegal.

LEARNING FROM MINNESOTA

Not all are happy with the tougher approaches being pressed for the protection of teachers. In March 2016, Minnesota State Senator Dave Brown introduced a bill that "would require school boards to automatically expel students who assault teachers by threatening or inflicting bodily harm. The board would also have the power to decide if and when those students can return, and place them in different classrooms."[24] This is called expulsion that is not really expulsion. But such a policy is a decent start.

Leaders and some educators from the St. Paul Federation of Teachers and elsewhere in the state are on record saying Brown's plan "would go against everything they've been fighting for . . . expanded support services for students to reduce disruptive behavior and improve school safety."[25] The leaders of the federation appear more concerned with programs of restorative justice than protection of teachers, thinking that more district resources are the way to assist students, versus expulsion. Decision-makers who form programs tend to miss the mark in the application of programs. In this case, it is the mission of protecting people that misses the mark.

There was other disagreement over Brown's bill. From the vantage points of some Minnesota teachers, Brown's bill requiring expulsion "increases the likelihood of dropping out of school—and committing future crimes. Racially biased expulsions also hurt students' higher education prospects, as colleges and universities increasingly consider disciplinary records during the admissions process."[26]

In Brown's defense, and in the defense of teachers not sharing the federation's perspective, the senator argues: "Imagine if you're a teacher in a public school and you're assaulted, I mean physically violently assaulted by a student, and that student's going to be coming back. I think every teacher should have that right to determine whether they want that student back in their classroom or not . . . they may say no, I'm fearful of that student."[27]

Brown's bill was a reaction to the problems of school dangers. Just three months prior to Brown's bill, the St. Paul teachers threatened to go on strike because of the violence in the district against teachers. According to Denis Specht, the president of Education Minnesota since 2013, "Every teacher . . . either has had a physical confrontation with a student or has a colleague who has. . . . School safety has become a major issue statewide."[28]

In another instance, just a week prior to the introduction of Brown's bill, Candice Egan accepted a substitute position at the St. Paul Creative Arts Secondary School. Egan claimed she was told by staff that a particular after lunch class was extremely challenging. Once class began, the problems between students accelerated. One student refused to hand over his smartphone, swore at Egan, and threatened her.

Eventually Egan commandeered the smartphone and the student pushed Egan against a window and hit her repeatedly. When Egan attempted to dial the school office on the classroom phone, the student in question hung up the phone. When she was finally able to regain her composure, Egan was able to get through to the school office and was told they were unable to help her.

Egan filed an injury report, which set in motion actions by the St, Paul school district, teacher's federation, and the state of Minnesota.[29]

Imagine if the Minnesota money was dedicated for STEM academics, or to work with the troubled students at an alternative/continuation campus, rather than at the site where the student committed an assault. How does this help teachers feel safer? What message does it send to students who are behavior compliant, or those whose actions are not chronic behavior problems?

The issue here is not whether a school district is actually providing more and more services to help students. The issue is whether the schools are using their existing resources effectively and removing the violent students from classrooms. Teachers must fight the underlying policies that keep violent students in their classrooms.

SOCIAL JUSTICE AND ZERO TOLERANCE

Politicians and special interest groups are often swayed by ideology. Social justice programs are the result of a certain sway. Social and restorative justice programs have been embedded in many schools' practices. However, when the programs are used as a means to enable troubled students to remain matriculated, or after others commit violent assaults, then the policy places teachers and students at risk.[30] Social justice should apply to all.

Restoration should not have as its only goal the re-matriculation of the offender. If this happens, then what is lost in the equation is the restoration of the relationship between the offender and the teacher he or she assaults, as well as the class in which the assault occurred. Add to this also the impacts on the psyches of the schoolwide community. When classroom injustice results, social justice has failed.

Americans must decide if their public schools are a hospital for emotionally ill, violent, or desperate and angry young people, or whether they are places of academics. There is a conflict for teachers. Teachers are standing up against violence they experience, yet keeping the violent students among them risks greater harm and provides less focus on academics. It reduces schools to institutions of racial and social justice, rather than institutions of intellectual and academic justice for those families seeking the best for their own children.[31] How is a program of social justice the *just* thing for the masses affected by the actions of others?

Second and Third Chances

Second and third chances exist for students. They should have to earn their ways back into the good graces of schooling. This should happen over time and not at the same school where the offenses were committed. If students refuse to focus on academics, should the schools then try to save the students from themselves? The older the child, the more difficult these efforts become.

Many good-hearted teachers have a knack for seeing the obvious and moving it into the category of the oblivious, especially during difficult encounters with students. They just move on and compartmentalize. It is at this point that an assault may have damaged the very soul of the teacher—the seat from which the ultimate passion is derived—resulting in the incremental spiritual and psychological loss of another from the profession. Just one basic and sensible truism is applicable here. Even though not all beatings are the same, they are beatings nonetheless. They all hurt.

Extract Violent Students

There will never be a school where safety concerns do not exist. But they can be minimized by extraction. Removing students who have clearly demonstrated violence sends the message that safety is of great importance, not only for teachers, but also for the assaulting students. Schools are not meant to be war zones.

Schools are meant to be institutions of learning and academic preparation, so that students can one day make a difference in the world. Arriving at this end goal is next to impossible if violence or fear are in the way of advancing toward its fulfillment. It can never occur if teacher turnover remains high. With these things in mind, it appears that states like Minnesota are heading in reverse.

In terms of Minnesota's Federation of Teachers, an agreement was reached with the state in early 2017 to invest nearly $5 million dollars in "restorative justice practices." According to the executive director of the Minnesota Association of School Administrators, "Every time you have a situation, there are circumstances that we believe need to be taken into account: the age of the student, the background of the student, the discipline record of the student, is the student dealing with special needs?"[32]

The interesting aspect here is that the state legal and penal systems are not so forgiving of crimes. But they first have to be reported, and this is half the battle. Keeping teachers in schools while they lack the necessary support is the other half of the battle.

DISCIPLINE POLICY FAILURE

The discipline being meted out for violent expressions by students is often to keeping students out of class for a time, or placing them on in-school suspension. These actions often are not officially written up as suspensions. As an example of the rising frustrations, a recent special education teacher reached out and shared his concerns.

> Recently it seems that it is becoming more the expectation that special educators will be injured on the job, and furthermore we should not complain or file accident reports. I am CPI trained and have never had to use restraint until this year. I avoid it even to getting injured myself. However when injured I will file a report. Personally I think that the student and the teacher have equal rights to be safe in the classroom setting. If restraint has to be used repeatedly shouldn't a behavior manifestation meeting be held? . . . Are other special ed. teachers getting hurt on the job?[33]

Teachers Going the Extra Mile

Codes of Education in some states seem to favor special education and special needs students explicitly over other students. Specifically, these students may be treated differently if they act out violently and assault teachers or other students, or endanger others at school.

According to Adam Clark, associate superintendent of educational services, California's Education Code requires that "If a student in special education goes on the attack, employees in that program are first required to ensure that the school is providing the additional services he or she needs to determine whether the student's disability was a contributing factor to the violence. . . . In the case of a child who is impulsive to the point that his lack of self-control is a disability . . . advising expulsion might be less desirable than transferring him to another campus."[34]

Parents deserve to know their children are safe at school. Teachers are beginning to express concern that adding special needs students to their classrooms is adding greater risk of harm. But special needs students are not the only concern. According to some teachers classrooms are unsafe, and hostile work environments exist for a variety of reasons.

Administrators that tend to make promises to deal with the violence, yet do not follow through to support their teachers, frustrate teachers and parents. Teachers clamor for fair but *just* policies. They must continue to fight against policies that weaken their abilities to do their jobs.

ZERO TOLERANCE POLICIES

The problems associated with zero tolerance classroom policies are that they often yield more formal written disciplinary actions on the parts of administrators. This is only a problem for those seeking to make their schools look good. Yet the removal of zero tolerance policies, in the midst of more and more violence in schools, is not the right answer. Such a removal is a political and empathetic response to a set of cultural, family, and moral problems.

To what extent, if any, should schools become the students' parents? This question is still being asked in education circles and, depending on the nature of the elected officials, the answers will differ.

One thing is certain. Removing the zero tolerance policy in order to make it appear that there are less problems within classrooms, means teachers must tolerate sometimes shocking surges in student violence and abuse. It also means that new discipline programs must be developed and deployed to intervene and adjust behaviors before students lash out. Motivation for keeping or removing zero tolerance policies is key. If schools are the new definitions of families, the families are in desperate need of intervention.

Some schools are beginning to take on the microcosmic appearance of prisons. They are finding ways to intervene in the cycles of violence and trying to get at the root causes of anger and rage, which develop into students' lashing out. This means that schools are becoming known as rehabilitation centers. How ironic would it be if the *prison* nickname students gave high school long ago became a self-fulfilling prophecy?

Is There Any Balance?

Some view the disability or the disorder of a student as justification not to apply a zero tolerance policy. So many things trigger students in a normal classroom environment that outbursts are not relegated to one or two occasions. Adding to this is an increase in class sizes by the addition of mainstreamed special education students.

Asking teachers to maintain decorum, and manage each student's classroom behaviors, while taking care not to focus on formal discipline of students from traditional minority groups, is highly problematic. Where is the balance? Things become exponentially more problematic with increased class sizes. Imbalanced classes, with some imbalanced students, do not make for balanced working conditions.

Arguments for and against Zero Tolerance

There are some excellent arguments for and against zero tolerance of violence against teachers. An argument against zero tolerance is that the student should not always be held accountable for his or her violent actions. Circumstances may have occurred in the student's life, so holding the student legally responsible for his or her actions would demonstrate a lack of empathy and be a disincentive toward providing help for the student.

Proponents of the zero tolerance policy of violence against teachers argue that, in order to protect teachers from other violence, people must be held accountable for their actions, which might include an arrest. Either way, each situation has to be dealt with, considering all the parties involved.

Recently, arguments for and against zero tolerance for violence were debated after an incident involving a local high school math teacher. The question was raised about the extent the student was to be held accountable and the extent the teacher assumed some culpability in his own assault. As the in-class situation unfolded, a teacher and student got involved in an argument. The teacher was punched in the face during class by the angry student.

The teacher was knocked unconscious and suffered serious facial and eye injuries. The incident was hushed at the school level and reported to the district office. The media never heard about this beating and the teacher returned to class within a few days, still bearing a swollen face and blackened eyes. The student was eventually transferred to another school and matriculated and graduated from the new school.

This is not a good example of how teacher assaults should be handled. Regardless of one's position on zero tolerance, there should be agreement on one thing. The agreement should be that weak school policies and weak enforcement of a weak policy will never prove to be a deterrent to poor behavior by students. Such weaknesses will never bode well for reducing violence against teachers, and they certainly do not create the workplace incentive for teachers to consider career longevity.

STANDING UP AND FIGHTING BACK

Those who are members of the NEA are finding that additional attention is bringing added protections in their favor. Even so, the question persists: *What are teachers to do when an assault occurs?* If they are members of their teachers' association, the following actions can be taken on their behalf. Even teachers who are not members have protections through their collectively bargained agreements with their districts.

Teachers should check with their local or site association representatives for complete details on how to file a report of an assault, and the steps to be taken subsequent to the filing. Teachers should also refer to their collective bargaining agreements, or contracts, to understand the processes by which reports must be filed, who should be informed, and when to file an official grievance if the administrators on campus fail to perform their duties to protect the teachers and make the campus safe.

The NEA provides a list of measures to take, in terms of protections for teachers:[35]

- Local districts should argue for language in the collective bargaining agreements "recognizing the employees' right to a safe working environ-

ment, including the right to be free from threats of violence from students."[36]
- If weak or unsupportive administrators "fail to take action to remove the threat (e.g., by returning the student to class) then the association could file a grievance and perhaps take it to arbitration."[37]
- The local association, along with supportive community members, should "lobby the school district to adopt policies and a protocol giving staff specific guidance for dealing with disruptive and violent students,"[38] which also means regular in-services and professional development, given the nature of some special needs students being mainstreamed.
- The NEA has developed a Safe Schools Program, through the Health Information Network, which can help to deal with various aspects associated with school violence.[39]

Another thing that teachers can do to regain a semblance of command in the profession is to call for the end of emotional promotions. This is addressed in the following section.

Regaining Educational Focus

In order to unite students, there first has to be a *common sense of purpose*. In many ways, America has lost its way in education, seeking to be all things to all people, and all expressions to all identities. In order to regain our education goal, our nation's schools must first refocus on students and their academic learning.

There is a job to do in educating young people to one day take over from the adults. To move in that direction, Americans must first minimize social engineering and political expediency, on behalf of their students. Taking a stand for academics is something teachers are enjoined to undertake. This is what reignites passion. The passion for teaching and the excitement of making a difference in student learning is why teachers entered the profession in the first place. Far too much is pressing teachers to leave their passion behind and work elsewhere.

Second, Americans must stand against the attempts of factions, intent on separating us into marginalized groups. Whether left or right, Americans must not allow efforts to undermine the values of our nation, its communities, and families. Americans, like the rest of the world, understand that the family is the bedrock of any society. Families must be supported so that they will begin to respect schools again.

The reasons some battles are being engaged in is that they have little to nothing to do with academics and everything to do with a political and social agenda. Tensions remain high. For all the time, money, and effort invested in Common Core, and now the ESSA, what does the nation have to show for the investment? Ideologies and ideologues come and go. The problem is that each cycle takes with it more and more of the soul of education.

Third, schools should not be places of social and moral experimentation, motivated by filling the very vacuum created by themselves. Certain social militancy naturally leads to violence. The Antifa groups that have sprung up at rallies and in cities are good examples of violence stemming from this militancy. The ideas have a receptive breeding ground in America's schools and colleges.

Fourth, teachers serve their students best when their focus is on the academic and skills training of the next generation. Anything that rivals academics and preparation for the future success of students is best left to families, places of worship, community organizations, and other local organizations.

Next, needless money is spent on the newest and latest educational fads. Veteran teachers are well aware that there really is nothing completely new finding its way into classrooms in the United States. Whether the supposed newest notion of doing away with D or F grades is deemed the most innovative idea for teachers, or smart veteran teachers are being told the latest version of psychology in the classroom comes by way of a revolutionary new program, savvy teachers understand there is nothing new under the sun.

Last, consider the supposed newest educational kid on the block: Social-Emotional Learning (SEL). This is actually not something new, but a repackaging of several older and already tried groups of methods to get students to behave and act in accordance with traits and values.[40] SEL is different in at least one way, though. It is broader than the older programs and promotes itself as interventions and strategies for increased learning. Teachers have been doing this for years, intuitively.[41]

Many younger advocates refer to SEL as the best way to promote learning in the classroom. Veterans have seen fads come and go.[42] The fact is that when something in education becomes programmatic it tends to lose its intuitive impact. Critics and veteran teachers refer to SEL as another repackaging of the "flawed California self-esteem movement"[43] of a few decades ago. We need to do better. We must do better!

REVERSING THE TREND

The word *change* has a nice ring to it. Certainly, there are many connotations associated with change. Aside from any political, colloquial axiom, what change denotes, in terms of today's educational crises in education, is something much more practical.

America has changed much in the last decade. As a nation, we are more marginalized across culture, race, ethnicity, gender, and a host of other categories. Caught up in this marginalization are the students. What affects students outside of school is always brought with them to school.

Students receive special protections that marginalize them. Teachers are marginalized by administrators and parents. There is great disparity between the levels of protection afforded students, and those afforded teachers. Teachers sense this lack of protection and support. This is another reason that convincing teachers to stay on the job is becoming more and more difficult. Where is the change?

Teachers are calling for change to reverse the trend of *soft* treatment of students who disrupt the educational process for other students. Some states are catching on as teachers fight for this change. Teachers are experiencing more reasons not to remain as teachers. But states are demonstrating support with the hope that such support not only protects teachers but reverses disincentives for teachers to remain in the classrooms.

In reversing the trend of the teacher exodus, state leaders must learn from the successes and failures of neighboring states. For example, any race-based discipline policy, or policy that is based on physical externals and not behaviors, is probably akin to profiling. State or federal discipline policies based on anything other than behaviors is off the mark today, causes fear of action, and certainly is not an attractive incentive for the average person thinking about a teaching career.

NOTES

1. Nick Morrison. "Don't write off teachers just yet—they are more important than ever." *Forbes*. February 28, 2017. Retrieved from https://www.forbes.com/sites/nickmorrison/2017/02/28/dont-write-off-teachers-just-yet-they-are-more-important-than-ever/#334d4d1c1a0a.

2. Stephen Wall. "Is housing built for teachers a solution to California's staffing shortage?" *The Press Enterprise*. July 2, 2017. Retrieved from http://www.pe.com/2017/07/02/bill-would-help-pay-for-teacher-housing/.

3. Elizabeth Behrman. "Many Harrisburg teachers resign over student violence." *Pittsburgh Post-Gazette*. November 26, 2017. Retrieved from http://www.post-gazette.com/news/education/2017/11/22/Harrisburg-teachers-union-resign-student-violence-classroom-school-district-discipline/stories/201711220161.

4. Editors. "Curbing classroom violence [editorial]." *The Baltimore Sun*. February 17, 2014. Retrieved from http://www.baltimoresun.com/news/opinion/editorial/bs-ed-suspensions-20140217-story.html.

5. Jennifer Fink. "Safe comfortable housing out of reach for many teachers." *We Are Teachers*. November 17, 2017. Retrieved from https://www.weareteachers.com/reality-home-ownership-for-teachers/?utm_content=1511113027&utm_medium=social&utm_source=twitter.

6. Erin Cox. "State to investigate allegations of grade tampering in Prince George's." *The Baltimore Sun*. June 28, 2017. Retrieved from http://www.baltimoresun.com/news/maryland/education/bs-md-pg-graduation-rate-investigation-20170628-story.html.

7. Sascha Brodsky. "Is discipline reform really helping decrease school violence?" *The Atlantic*. June 28, 2016. Retrieved from https://www.theatlantic.com/education/archive/2016/06/school-violence-restorative-justice/488945/.

8. Jose Sepulveda. "California bans travel to Texas and 3 other states." *AOL News*. June 23, 2017. Retrieved from https://www.aol.com/article/news/2017/06/23/california-bans-travel-to-texas-and-3-other-states/22584249/.

9. Ibid.

10. Michael D. Simpson. "What NEA affiliates are doing to protect members from violent and disruptive students." July 12, 2017. National Education Association. Retrieved from http://www.nea.org/home/42238.htm. See also *National Education Association Health Information Network: Safe Schools Program*. Retrieved from http://www.neahin.org/programs/schoolsafety/resources.

11. Ibid.
12. Ibid.
13. Ibid.
14. Ibid.
15. Ibid.
16. Ibid.

17. Jason Molinet. "L.I. teacher Catherine Engelhardt knocked out by irate mom in hallway beatdown at Hempstead middle school: Cops." *New York Daily News*. April 17, 2015. Retrieved from http://www.nydailynews.com/news/crime/teacher-choked-punched-kicked-irate-mom-cops-article-1.2188560.

18. Ibid.
19. Ibid
20. Ibid.

21. Simpson. "What NEA affiliates are doing to protect members."

22. Ibid.
23. Ibid.

24. Carimah Townes. "Even teachers who have personally been assaulted oppose harsh new Minnesota bill." *Think Progress*. March 30, 2016. Retrieved from https://thinkprogress.org/even-teachers-who-have-personally-been-assaulted-oppose-harsh-new-minnesota-bill-c2e044d7a359.

25. Ibid
26. Ibid.
27. Ibid.

28. James Walsh. "St. Paul teachers threaten strike over school violence." *Star Tribune*. December 10, 2015. Retrieved from http://www.startribune.com/silva-to-address-questions-of-teacher-safety-and-union-s-request-for-mediation/361318431/.

29. Dionne Cordell-Whitney. "Teacher claims she lost work after student's assault." *Courthouse News Service*. December 23, 2016. Retrieved from http://www.courthousenews.com/teacher-claims-she-lost-work-after-students-assault/.

30. Kristin Anderson Moore. "Defining the term 'at-risk.'" *Child Trends*. October 2006. Retrieved from https://www.childtrends.org/wp-content/uploads/2006/01/DefiningAtRisk1.pdf.

31. Brenda Isaacs. "High school district policy raises questions." *The Bakersfield Californian*. November 21, 2017, p. 21.

32. Townes. "Even teachers who have personally been assaulted oppose harsh new Minnesota bill."

33. K. S. Special Educator: 4th–5th Full Inclusion. "Getting injured part of the 'job' or not." *Edutopia*. May 2, 2017. Retrieved from https://www.edutopia.org/groups/special-ed/18077.

34. Rowena Coetsee. "Antioch: 13-year-old girl cited for beating middle-school teacher." February 4, 2017. *Mercury News*. Retrieved from http://www.mercurynews.com/2017/02/02/antioch-punishing-students-for-big-offenses-can-be-complicated/.

35. Simpson, "What NEA affiliates are doing to protect members."

36. Ibid.
37. Ibid.
38. Ibid.
39. Ibid.

40. Frederick Hess. "Some advice for champions of social and emotional learning." *Education Next*. December 13, 2017. Retrieved from http://educationnext.org/advice-champions-social-emotional-learning/.
41. Ibid.
42. Ibid.
43. Chester E. Finn. "Why are schools still peddling the self-esteem hoax?" *Education Week*. June 19, 2017. Retrieved from http://www.edweek.org/ew/articles/2017/06/21/why-are-schools-still-peddling-the-self-esteem.html.

Chapter Four

Classroom Management and Teacher Support

> School violence in general and its aftermath continue to be significant problems for students, teachers, staff, and schools. Most scholars agree that school violence is a multi-systemic problem.[1]

Most teachers in public schools say they are working harder than ever. Well-meaning administrators have assured teachers that if a new program is to be added to the workload of already overburdened teachers something will also be removed. Rarely does this assurance ever come to fruition. Universally, today's teachers are expected to necessitate good classroom instruction *and* classroom management. These are the basic, or primary, elements that a teacher is expected to possess at the time of hire, and to refine throughout the course of a career.

CLASSROOM BEHAVIOR MANAGEMENT STRATEGIES

The basic or primary elements of classroom management include (1) planning of lessons, (2) duplicating assignment papers, (3) grading and keeping track of student progress, which usually is posted online, (4) communicating with parents, which becomes more laborious in junior high and high school, (5) learning new curriculum programs through professional development, and (6) discipline and intervention strategies.

What many who are not in the trenches daily do not realize is that the aforementioned basic elements are also inseparably partnered to secondary and tertiary elements. Many of these other elements are somehow left out of teacher training and often experienced first. The basic elements expected of teachers soon fade into the background as the daily regimen shifts to secondary and tertiary classroom concerns. This is part of the confusion for newer teachers and why they feel overburdened.

Along with confusion and frustration, there is also desperation. Underqualified and unprepared teachers deal with the reality that is thrust upon them. The gap between what is expected and the feeling of being overwhelmed is sometimes the impetus for younger teachers to leave the classroom within the first three years on the job.

Challenges to Classroom Management

Whatever idealism the new teacher brings to his or her first teaching job is quickly tempered by the immediate challenges. Practicality supplants ideology and teachers must make this shift. The real world of teaching has real people with real issues. To be fair, the real world also contains wonderful challenges that await and moments of exhilaration for newer teachers and veterans alike. These also must be experienced to be fully understood.

Challenges to twenty-first-century American public schools now include the emotionally and mentally disturbed in regular classrooms. There are also children affected by drugs before birth. Foster and homeless children, who have been abused and are sometimes physically violent themselves, are in seats waiting to learn. There are also a variety of special needs children mixed in and mainstreamed with other students. The challenges present themselves very quickly and classroom management is front and center in ways it was not just a few years ago.

Addressing this reality is not some zealous diatribe against students. Understanding reasons why some teachers leave the profession they once loved, and the ways to stop this migration, means addressing the obvious yet often unspoken elements. The truth is that the challenges for all teachers today are greater than many have experienced in their careers.

Over the course of nearly forty years in education, students' faces, names, and many of their struggles continue to remind the heart of this veteran teacher of the work that still needs to be accomplished. However, something has taken place in American public education, and the changes are as unfathomable as the direction is unmistakable. If the veteran teacher feels overwhelmed and underqualified, then there should be nothing but understanding and empathy directed towards newer teachers experiencing the same.

Dedication and Persistence

One of the most wonderful traits possessed by dedicated teachers is their persistence. Educators rarely give up on children—even when children have given up on themselves. In some ways, and aside from parenting, teaching is a job that presses most teachers up to the edge of unconditional acceptance.

Therefore, in this quasi-teacher-parent amalgam, how well teachers care for those with varying degrees of disability is as unconditional as it gets.

However, this same unconditional acceptance also extends to *all* students throughout a regular school day. In the real world, the concept of *educational equity* appears more sensible in the abstract, yet comes with the expectation of application on a regular basis. The fact is that all students desire the same equity and acceptance.

Across the nation, teachers are frustrated with the inability to maintain control over some of the behaviors of some of their students. Some students are affecting the learning environment so drastically that removal of one or more students for a day is like a breath of fresh air for a teacher and the other students.

Does unconditional acceptance also come with an understanding and acceptance by students of the discipline meted out to them? In the middle of all of the discourse on acceptance, the real world is again calling the willing to action. But the question is, *what action should be taken?*

IS CORPORAL PUNISHMENT THE ANSWER?

Incidents of students getting physical are sometimes finding their way into daily discipline reports. In some cases the reports are so frequent that there has been a surge in community discussions as to whether bringing back using corporal punishment in schools might help. Florida is one state questioning whether corporal punishment is an answer to the discipline problems.

Reports from law enforcement in Pinellas County show pushing and hitting teachers is on the rise. In fact, "this kind of incident happens regularly. One teacher told officers violence at the school is out of hand and that students think hitting and shoving teachers is OK. Another teacher said the physical aggression by students is unlike anything he's ever seen before."[2]

Mike Gandolfo of the Pinellas Classroom Teachers Association says: "this kind of thing happens all too often . . . administrators are fearful of losing their jobs. Incidents like these do not look good on reviews, so they don't write them up."[3] This raises the question as to whether corporal punishment is the answer.

There remain nineteen states that still allow paddling of students for misbehavior. The Supreme Court left the decision to the states as to disciplining students in their public schools. This allowance extends also to caregivers. At the time of this writing, the nineteen states that "allow teachers and caregivers to spank children (and administer other forms of corporal punishment),"[4] include (1) Alabama, (2) Arizona, (3) Arkansas, (4) Colorado, (5) Florida, (6) Georgia, (7) Indiana, (8) Iowa, (9) Kansas, (10) Kentucky,

(11) Louisiana, (12) Missouri, (13) Montana, (14) North Carolina, (15) Oklahoma, (16) South Carolina, (17) Tennessee, (18) Texas, and (19) Wyoming.

Assaults Still Occur

Even with the threat of corporal punishment at these nineteen schools, there are still assaults on teachers. As a form of discipline, spanking does not appear to dissuade students from violence, especially if administered when emotions are running high. Spanking might produce the opposite of the intended effect, in these cases. There is literature on both sides of this argument. However, there is one point of agreement for all sides in the corporal punishment debate. That is spanking a 6-foot 2-inch sixteen-year-old is probably not a good idea, and for obvious reasons.

The best disciplinary actions come from home. However, corporal punishment, if administered at school, often brings mixed messages. Along with these mixed messages are clear messages that result in lawsuits. As Rose Eveleth, a writer for *Smart News*, concludes: "What parents do in their homes and what teachers do in school are two different things. But there are parents who wouldn't hit their kids at home, who are also sending them to schools where their teachers can do just that."[5] Is this an example of the best of *both worlds*, or just some examples of inconsistency and intolerance?

States like Tennessee are considering a revision of their corporal punishment policies and practices. For example, in Hamilton County, "the district recorded 270 instances of corporal punishment, with a single school accounting for 69 percent."[6] The district is opting for a social-emotional program that it feels better addresses the needs of students.[7]

The sensible question to ask is whether corporal punishment is administered as a reaction to an incident or as a correction to a behavior. If it is being administered in the former case, it is on behalf of the teacher. If administered for the latter, it is applied as a correction to a student's behavior. The ultimate concern is the students and what is best for them, without compromising the teachers' authority.

WELFARE OF THE TEACHER

What gets lost in the shuffle of politically based social programs for students is the welfare of teachers. Teachers are directly in the line of fire of students' outbursts of anger. The public is becoming more aware of the violence that goes on at schools, and they are becoming more vocal about it.

Smartphones have helped users find immediate audiences. But such information distribution is more gossipy than anything else. Violence against teachers is a serious matter. Not until the issue receives the legal attention it deserves will it become front and center enough for bureaucrats and politicians to do something about it.

Fearful of Fallout

Bureaucrats fear attention from constituent parents. They do not fear teachers as much. One reason is that parents go to the media, while teachers bring concerns to their administrators. Today's parents tend to pounce on superintendents. They go right to the top. The media delve into stories of teachers being assaulted, and declare the existence of unsafe schools. These stories tend to take on lives of their own.

The political fallout of a teacher assaulted on his or her campus is serious political business. Aside from the gossip of *supposed* incidents that occur on campuses, there are many accounts that go unreported. There is no bureaucrat—and certainly no superintendent—who is dictating that all reports of assaults on campus should involve official reports and police engagement. Making waves is not an administrator's first choice.

Make No Waves

Given reports of unsafe schools, what school principal could hope to rise through the ranks in a district, with the media hounding him and printing articles about controversies that arise at schools he oversees? Likewise, what teachers would be appointed as principals, or district-level administrators, after they filed grievances with their districts over being assaulted, or complaining about hostile workplaces? The chances of advancement or promotion are slim in the face of such victimization.

The Kern High School District, the largest high school district in the state of California, recently lost a lawsuit due to what civil rights and social justice groups perceived as an inordinate number of black and Hispanic students being disciplined, suspended, or expelled from the district's eighteen comprehensive high schools. Court decisions such as these have led schools all over California, as well as in other parts of the nation, to tolerate behaviors and overlook other behaviors that, in the past, would have removed students from schools.

Bureaucracy Diminishes Classroom Management

Many are left to wonder whether bureaucracy has made schools less safe,[8] thereby diminishing classroom management for teachers. Does anyone besides civil rights factions and their attorneys really think teachers practice selective discipline based on skin color? Do Americans really believe classroom teachers target students for discipline in this way? This type of accusation levied upon teachers does not provide an incentive for new teachers to join the profession, and it is an unfair characterization. It certainly does little to retain veteran teachers.

Another situation arose at a secondary school in the aforementioned district, where a teacher and a student became involved in a fistfight during a class. The assault was begun by the student and security was called. Security refrained from initial intervention, because students were recording the violent altercation on their cell phones.

This story never hit the media. It was apparently too toxic, since it deals with a student of a protected group in California, and because the student had already been removed from one high school because of violence and placed in another. Stories like these get buried under the protective wing of "personnel issues." If administrators cannot manage their schools, how can they expect teachers to manage their classrooms?

Interestingly enough, the recordings of the incident mentioned above were mysteriously kept from being posted on social media pages. It was clear from witnesses that the student assaulted the teacher, which prompted the entire incident.

EQUITY MINDEDNESS

Cheryl Ching recently completed her dissertation at the University of Southern California. Her topic was educational equity. She served as a research fellow at the university. Ching had been funded by the Bill and Melinda Gates Foundation and currently works in conjunction with *USC's Center for Urban Education* (CUE).

Although her research is pertinent to higher education, it has implications for K–12. When asked about why race is fundamental to equity-minded thinking, she replied:

> All too often, talk about students is in the aggregate. Our students are engaged. Our students are learning. Our students are not learning. But CUE tries to disrupt that thinking by asking, Who are you talking about when you say *students*? Who do you imagine when you say *students*? When you say that your teaching works for students, which students are we actually talking about? In particular, CUE tries to get practitioners to think about whether and how teaching, advising and other practices work for African-Americans, Latinx and other racially minoritized students. . . . So the question becomes, how does a practice work for an African-American student, a Latinx student?[9]

Ching's statement separates students into categories, and she seems to view them as entities. This makes more sense in sociology, with demographic studies, and the like. Should this categorization be applied to students in public schools, and should teachers view students in these ways? What are the implications, and should teachers be trained to think about the racial makeups of their students before each lesson?

Teachers would be so constrained by focusing on race in order to reach an outcome for one group that they might unintentionally disenfranchise others. This is an example of focusing on a secondary element in education. How long will it be before parents feel their children are either profiled or left out for questionable reasons?

The energies that go into these types of secondary elements in most public school classrooms, especially at the elementary level, occupy most of an elementary teachers' time. Teachers today must be so much more than communicators of knowledge and purveyors of learning.

Monitoring and regulating students in a myriad of ways is quickly becoming a new norm for teachers. If those serving in urban education have their way, lesson preparation may have to include the consideration of goals and curriculum along with a student's race. This is not so far-fetched. Although it sounds fair-minded, teachers should focus on academic needs over the race or ethnicity of their students. Classroom management is now so much more than instructional methodologies and checking for understanding, as Ching's study demonstrates.

In terms of instruction, whether the issue is Common Core Math, Language Arts, NextGen Science, a new Social Studies curriculum, an elective, or anything else that is expected to be taught and assessed in today's public school classrooms, teachers must also be making adjustments. One would be hard-pressed to find another profession that endures changes so very often, confusing laborers and constituents alike in the process.

There is a very real sense about modern educational change. That is, this change is often for the sake of political or bureaucratic decisions. All bureaucratic decisions must be challenged on the basis of whether the decisions are for the sake of making schools safer and better places for learning for all students and families. Would potential teacher education students find enough incentive in this reality to flock to education training institutions and be compelled to join the ranks?

THE CHALLENGES ARE REAL

Teachers must constantly challenge themselves to discover new ways to make sense to students with various learning challenges. New curricula added into the mix only make the challenges greater, for both teachers and students. In addition to new classroom rosters each year, teachers find it unreliable to count on last year's educational methods and content. Education shifts quickly, and sometimes these shifts feel like the irreversible pull of an ocean's receding water on the shoreline.

Despite facing near-impossible odds, the classroom intangibles elicit an amazing reservoir of teachers' reserves and a remarkable resilience. That being said, teachers run on fumes more days than not, and still have some left to give. However, these types of challenges alone are presently diminishing incentives for even the most resilient of teachers to remain in the profession. Replacing those with the values and motivation just described are not successful—especially if they sense there is little support from administrators to assist them when needed.

Students Have Challenges to Their Learning

More students who have serious learning issues are attending public schools. This is a serious test for all teachers and their classroom management skills. The expectation is that teaching more and teaching better will somehow overcome the learning disabilities of a good number of students in many classes. One wonders at the fallout resulting from the collision between the philosophical and the practical. On the one hand, the expectation is in the backs of teachers' minds. On the other hand, reality is directly before them.

Moving more slowly to accommodate all the learners in today's schools is questionable progress at best. Moving in multiple directions simultaneously means less teaching and more student independent work. At this point teachers are facilitators. When was the last time the readers came across positions for elementary school facilitators? Teachers teaching less and facilitating more is not what teacher training institutions are preaching. This can only add to great challenges for education at large.

Changing curriculum, adjusting its levels of difficulty, or even revising educational standards is unlikely to change education status quo. America has changed and, for better or worse, is never going to recapture status as a nation known for elite K–12 education. Optimists would tell us differently, while money is poured into a seemingly bottomless pit.

The once-lauded American educational system that produced amazing advancements is but a vestige of the past. Frankly, there is this sense that the nation is far too fractured and far too disabled by politics and special interest groups to recover its proud status of educational excellence. These are the realities even before the classroom doors open for business.

Challenging the Past

The classic 1970s movie soundtrack from *The Way We Were* is a hauntingly familiar refrain. Who can forget Redford and Streisand? Many Americans lack the knowledge and understanding of America's past, which means the chances of learning from it are reduced.

Sadly, previous generations are not passing on the history of our nation. The result of schools avoiding history and social science, in lieu of raising test scores in mathematics and English, is a lack of understanding of history. This is sad for today's students. They are apathetic to the history of the nation, and rightly so.

Some of this apathy can be blamed on the system that causes school focus to divert to assessments. Other blame can be placed on students' lack of desire to read. There is plenty of blame to go around; it can go toward the teacher, whose lessons were boring and unengaging, or those who seek to blame the United States for most things wrong in the world.

Revising American History

Many history majors and history/social science educators mourn the loss of social studies teaching time in schools. Maintaining apathy about the past does nothing but enable dissension-oriented factions to continue to revise our nation's history to match their agenda. Teachers who love their content are disenchanted when what they hoped to teach is replaced by sociopolitical revisions. How is this attractive to the majority of teachers?

On the programmatic front, *No Child Left Behind*, *Race to the Top*, *Common Core*, and other programs did little to press American students into more competitive positions on the world's stage. If there is a contest of video games, or social media posts, American students might show up in the top five. High stakes assessments are gone for now. So, now what? At least under the ESSA, civic education is allowed to undergo a resurgence.

There are factions apologizing and challenging our nation's past, while others are running from it with breakneck political speed. Some are making every effort to replace and revise American history by condemnation and shame. How can we expect American students to love their nation when those training them teach to the contrary? Does this not contradict values of many of the children's parents?

In order for the nation to advance as a nation, there must be a national oneness rallying around this unity. Teaching the errors and national sins is one way to cause anger and protest. But what will then replace what becomes dismantled?

Dismantling history without concern for dismantling America leaves the nation in a weakened state, and absent a historical mooring. Groups on the left, in the center, and on the right politically are far too busy rallying around themselves to give this much thought. Groups display passion for causes. Self-benefit, elevation of self-adulation, and expressions emotional gratification have become a trio of intoxicants for many of Generation Z. For so many in this group, winning at all cost is the new *socio-edu-dysiac*.

EFFECTIVE CLASSROOM MANAGEMENT

Classroom management can be explained as a process by which teachers and schools create and maintain the environment that fosters learning and the behaviors that add to the learning environment for students in classrooms. The appropriate behaviors have often been tied to teachers having the ability to *control* their students, both individually and as they work in groups. Any change in the classroom environment that diminishes the learning environment should be modified and the distractions minimized for the benefit of everyone involved.

Classroom management, then, is an ongoing occurrence throughout the school day, and should never be held to some sort of quantification. Classroom management occurs simultaneously to all other aspects of classroom activity and is never static. For example, classroom management ranges from body language to expressions of personality and displays of empathy. Additionally, classroom management can take shape [10] in:

- creating an inviting environment,
- posting regular material on walls,
- making certain students are seated and on task,
- disciplining in ways that look more like coaching than discipline,
- motivating the often unmotivated,
- setting straight the unruly students,
- finding ways to get supplies to students who are without them, and
- investing passion and emotion into each and every student, their families, and their work, through interpersonal considerations.

Managing a classroom is exactly that: *Managing*. It is management from top to bottom, side to side, and sometimes taking control of the noise level in the classroom.[11] Many teachers have an aversion to noise from students. Classrooms should not always resemble libraries. Management skills help to shape and motivate students of all ages, all backgrounds, and all temperaments. The best managers are those with contagious enthusiasm and motivational spirits.

Managing by Motivation

Managing people must always come before managing the world of the people. One invests in lives; the other invests in control. Classroom management has elements of both, but is best accomplished without the additional element of disciplining unruly behaviors.

Without incentives, or without the necessary motivation to achieve, any academic work anticipated by the teachers is likely to fall short, or at least produce an in-class struggle for student work production. All that goes into working with dozens to hundreds of students a day is so much more than curriculum.

Teachers who are constantly looking over their shoulders while instructing, or have to bury recent physical pains and/or daily anguish caused by students, parents, social media interactions, are not going to be at their best. Consequently, the students will not receive the quality of education they deserve.

When teachers find inordinate attention given to issues outside their primary and secondary roles, something needs to be done and change needs to occur. Without the support from colleagues and administrators teachers retreat into a regimen and are on the fast-track toward counting the days or years until they can leave the classroom, or retire.

Managing Classrooms and Students

How teachers manage their classrooms and whether this management is an extension of personal skill sets is a constant challenge. First, teachers thrive on routines for success and sanity. Therefore, establishing routines is important for classroom success. For example, in middle school and high school, students present themselves differently than they do in elementary school. Any teacher would acknowledge that students are different according to the times of the day, or the class periods.

Teachers manage classes much differently before lunch than they do their classes after lunch. Certain subjects are also best taught during the morning hours, when student self-control and interest may be at their highest levels. Teachers must guard against too much structure and routine, and strive for balance. Too much structure may prove to be triggers for certain students, and just the mention of this probably stirs up memories of students' faces and names from years' past.

Second, after lunch, students may return to their respective classrooms with different frames of mind than they possessed during the morning hours. Teachers must adjust to this, because such resilience enables teachers to maintain their academic regimen. For example, students may have had arguments or fights during lunch. Adrenaline and emotions may be piqued, as students are asked to line up to return to the classroom. Texting or social media posts might extend or exacerbate heated conflict.

Conflict residuals always seem to enter the classrooms after lunches, with each presenting unique challenges for many classroom teachers. What is a teacher's policy for external conflicts that enter the internal environment of the classroom? What is the student response to the policy? The answers to these questions must be worked out by all teachers for their unique situations.

Third, teachers must do what they need to do to find success and achievement for themselves and their students. When it comes to teacher safety, however, they find they are often unable to do what they need to do to protect their classes and themselves. What then?

The reality is, teachers are constrained from acting for fear of reprisal or dismissal. They need their administrators and district-level professionals to step up and assist. But what if they do not act? Faculty should insist that school-site administrators move the issue of school safety to the top of the list of campus priorities. This must become a classroom management imperative and be brought up at staff meetings and at parent meetings, until action is taken.

Teachers who resort to self-defense, for example, would find they are placed on administrative leave, sent to a "rubber room," or dismissed outright. There is a bizarre irony here. Teachers are told to do what is necessary for success but are warned not to do what is ultimately necessary in protecting their livelihood. Teachers who sense the need to physically defend everything they do should consider spending their years in another profession.

Fourth, school boards need to step up and do what is needed for teachers, students, and the parents they represent. Not allowing teachers to protect themselves places them in precarious spots. The teachers know it and the students know it.

When students and parents make a fuss about a teacher's actions, the result is usually not one that favors the teacher. This lack of support detracts from the teacher's ability to manage the class. This lack of support is also demoralizing to teachers emotionally. What is even more demoralizing, if not humiliating, is the campus principal agreeing with the teacher on the one hand, and disagreeing with the teacher in private, to support a parent's complaint. This practice should not occur.

Fifth, for a teacher seeking to accomplish similar outcomes for all of her classes, rethinking of applicable strategies for better student learning has to be on the forefront of her mind. So, the first thing a teacher must do is gauge the class and manage the class that walks into the classroom. Since students are always in a state of flux, understanding their environment, biology, and other factors will enable adjustments to move past the distractions and disruptions that diminish academics.

Sixth, schools, through their principal and teacher committees, need to rethink their discipline strategies and take the focus off restorative justice as a primary motivator. The focus should shift to safety first. This is best accomplished before a school year begins, not during or at its end. Teachers are frazzled and tired at points throughout the year—but especially at the end of the year. They have had to put up with a year of frustrations. Any policy developed under those conditions is not going to come across as balanced, but probably more retributive.

Next, in connection with the sixth point, where violence has occurred, the focus on teacher and student safety should be the first priority. The reduction of referrals, so as to reflect fewer classroom problems, should not be a primary motivator. Schools are full of disciplinary issues that are never officially written up. This makes a principal look good. This makes a principal look good, but it makes teachers look and feel badly. It does little to lift the natures of all students to evidence their better angels. Such a practice also raises the levels of fear and likelihood of repeated offenses, even injuries, by not addressing the problems head-on and with authority.

If restoring students is the priority, and not the overall safety of students, the risks are greater for all. No one in education is against second chances. But the second chances should not be weighed against teachers as such, so that there is fear of being injured more seriously next time in class. A second chance for assault is not only unprofessional, it is unethical and dangerous.

Last, district administrators have to be bold enough to demonstrate to their communities that safety is of the utmost of importance. Administrators should be less worried about their jobs and reputations, and possibilities of moving up, than they should be about supporting students and teachers. One of the accusations levied against administrators is that they have forgotten what it is like to be in class day in and day out.

ADMINISTRATORS' EFFORTS

Sometimes, because administrators or principals have not spent any significant or recent time in teaching situations in classrooms, these education leaders do not experience the challenges associated with the changes in generations. Classroom cultures change and teachers understand and experience these changes more comprehensively than administrators.

Ignorance Is Not Bliss

The recent statement from a local secondary principal reflects these changes and the disconnection that often exists between the office staff and those in the classrooms every day. The administrator had to admit, "I have been out of the classroom for eighteen years and I am shocked at how much the students have changed in that time." This realization is a good thing. However, the lack of understanding tends to minimize the importance of connecting the dots of the difficulties of classroom management and places blame for emerging challenges in the laps of teachers.

If administrators at the district and school levels intend to keep their faculty, yet remain unaware of their daily emotional and physical struggles, then the chances are slim of achieving that goal. As a demonstration of the lack of understanding, administrators infuriate teachers by sending students back to class after very tumultuous outbursts, or physical altercations

Distant Administrators

Administrators become distant to their teachers and students by both the natural direction of their job requirements, as well as by choice. Although administrators' hands are sometimes tied from acting on behalf of teachers with difficult classes, more can always be done to assist teachers. Teachers being trained for the classrooms of today's America who feel unsupported are not long for the profession. Some administrators find creative ways to be quite helpful to teachers and do whatever they can to assist teachers. These administrators are to be applauded and celebrated. Most people want to work for these administrators and more of this type is needed.

Supportive and Effective Administrators

Supportive and effective administrators are attuned to their schools and student populations as instructional leaders. They are inclined toward selfless support of faculty. They possess servant's hearts in action. In more cases than not, the image is portrayed that administrators are *checked out*. Some portray the image they cannot be bothered due to meetings, and they state that classroom teachers should handle their own classroom management issues, rather than involve an administrator.

Is it wishful thinking to consider that boards of education might require administrators to regain touch with classrooms on their campuses? It would do wonders for the morale of teachers and students to enjoy the presence of the administrator as substitute for a lesson, periodically. Taking a yard duty, or bus duty, for a teacher here and there would give teachers a few extra minutes. Fifteen minutes for a teacher to gather their thoughts might be the make-or-break difference of the day.

Twenty-First-Century Administrators

Administrators who step in for teachers to take over classrooms for a block of time, or assist in the rooms, find time to leave their offices and stay in touch with the goings-on of the school. This is a plus and what should be expected of the twenty-first-century administrator. Principals then achieve a first-hand experience of what the teacher experiences.

Schools districts in states like California are now expecting administrators and/or principals to spend time as substitutes in the classrooms on some of their campuses. This approach will give teachers confidence in dealing with troubled students, because the result will be an understanding that their principals have their backs and are emotionally aware of what they are going through.

School administrators must be able to come to terms with understanding today's students and how they are vastly different than students of just a decade ago. Teacher longevity has become a serious issue in American public education. School leaders can bridge the gap between the two. As explained earlier, as well as in other chapters of this book, one of the reasons teachers are not remaining in the classroom, as they have in the past, is the lack of support they feel from administrators and colleagues. Careers are built with strong support networks.

IMPACT OF GENERATION Z AS TEACHERS

Now that Generation Z is entering the workforce and, assuming a good number will enter a teaching career, dedication to a career that lacks the purpose for which they trained will diminish quickly. A job that does not pay well and has all the makings of daily stressors without support, may yield the largest bailing on a profession in a lifetime. Gen Z's commitment to career choices will largely be dependent on the feelings of appreciation they glean from their work, and the level of happiness they derive from the daily regimen.

What Gen Z may be taught in teaching training institutions may not reflect the reality that today's teachers face in American public school classrooms. Ideology either clashes or meshes with practicality. One thing is certain, ideology eventually meets with reality, and no one knows this better than today's classroom teacher. The reality is that today's Gen Z students are neither compliant nor tolerant of ideology and theory that are contrary to their own version of practicality.

A greater challenge will be for teachers emerging from within this generation to fight the tendency to acquiesce or retreat from the expectations placed upon them. Will Gen Z teachers *tough out* the difficulties that come along with difficult students and challenging parents? If policies do not change to reflect greater support the likelihood of even greater teacher shortages increases.

RELUCTANCE IN DEALING WITH VIOLENCE

Actions being taken by states in reaction to assaults on teachers are very slowly gaining traction. Education moves more swiftly with judicial outcomes on its side. However, absent these legal decisions, according to the National Education Association, the "tragic crisis is not going away anytime soon. Part of this problem lies with school officials, many of whom lack the backbone to expel chronic offenders, or at least transfer them to more secure schools."[12] Another part of the problem is the fear of the very lawsuit that would bring the necessary changes.

As mentioned earlier, school boards and administrators are reluctant to suspend or expel students, given that these actions demonstrate that schools could be labeled "unsafe," and would reflect negatively on the administrators. The boards are mostly comprised of those fearing lawsuits by parents, and parents claim that student discipline should incorporate more social justice and restorative features than punishments for actions.

The Trump Administration is moving away from mandates handed down from the federal government by the Obama Administration. Trump's team is revisiting what many have called an unfair racial quota discipline policy for schools.[13] Agree or disagree, teachers have to stand up and be counted. One of the ways teachers are standing up and being counted is through their National Education Association affiliates.[14]

SUPPORTIVE LEADERSHIP

Discovering the strengths and weaknesses of school-site administrators is not difficult, especially if the leader has been in the district or on a particular campus for some time. Reputations speak loudly and are established quickly among staff members. Administrators today are naturally weakened by laws that protect students and parents over their own faculty and staff. One thing that is not weakened is leadership.

Although administrators' authority may be constrained, their personalities and interpersonal support can go a long way to providing stability through difficult circumstances and provide strength to both newer and seasoned faculty members. Administrators need to take more active roles in supporting teachers. The following sections address the shoulds and should nots of administrators.

The Shoulds of a School-Site Administrator/Principal

A school-site administrator, or principal, *should* make clear, from the first day of school, the authority given to the teachers, the issues that potentially exist in the classrooms, and what teachers can and cannot do about them, according to law. This information is critical for the administrator to communicate. It is also helpful for grade-level teams consisting of faculty, and for professional development teams by discipline. School counselors should also be enlisted to lay out what actions are appropriate and what actions are not, in terms of understanding and applying any new laws pertaining to students.

The principal *should* also speak privately with those teachers who are expecting very difficult classes, or step in to balance classes to provide the best opportunity for success. One caveat for newer teachers may prove helpful. There are many stories that are told to teachers newer to campuses, detailing the assignment of some of the school's most difficult students to the newest teachers on campus.

Some schools, and some teachers at certain schools, will have issues beyond anyone's comprehension. Some teachers welcome such challenges. Most probably do not. If an administrator demonstrates the strength to split up classes, even in the face of parental criticism, or because teachers request another, teachers should count themselves fortunate for such administrative strength.

The principal *should* avoid negativity and vindictiveness. Placing blame on his or her faculty for classroom issues that arise, especially if he or she has not stepped into the classroom to assist, or to find assistance for the teacher, *should* be avoided. There may be some principals who wish to move teachers out of their schools, and thereby make certain the classes they are assigned are more difficult than those assigned to other teachers. This is called *throwing the teacher under the school bus*, and happens periodically in schools in America.

As for any reports to the principal regarding violence against teachers:

> Principals, assistant principals, superintendents, and school board members and other leaders *should*, first of all, institute a thorough investigation into the facts surrounding allegations of violence directed toward educators. School leaders *should* take all necessary steps to respond privately and publicly in a supportive fashion to the affected teachers and *should* address larger school and community needs when violence is perpetrated against educators. . . . Research clearly indicates that teachers' perceptions of support from their school administrators are strong predictors of whether teachers choose to stay in their present school or seek to move to another site.[15]

The Should Nots of a School-Site Administrator/Principal

The vindictive principal is an example of what a school administrator *should not* be. An example of a vindictive principal is one who surrounds himself or herself with similar-minded staff for personal empowerment or professional benefit. When faculty finally speak up about such principals and their actions, usually one of two things will occur. First, there may be a mass exodus of teachers from the school. Some of this exodus is directly the result of the principal's vindictiveness. Other faculty leave because of their desire to avoid the messy situation created by the principal.

Second, the vindictive principal's supportive inner-cadre might circle the wagons and create a hostile work environment behind the scenes. This usually forces out the person who issues an original report against some actions or inactions of the principal. Either way, good teachers are lost to the profession by vindictive principals, and the nation can ill afford to have this happen any longer.

In an example that hits close to home, one local principal was demoted because of the hostile and vindictive environment created at a local high school. True to form, a mass exodus of teachers to other schools resulted from the actions of a principal and his staff. The principal was eventually demoted and reassigned within the school district, when a detailed investigation determined that allegations against him turned out to be accurate. These allegations included, "a pattern of . . . bullying, gender discrimination and changing grades. An investigator also found "allegations of retaliation for participating in a sexual harassment investigation."[16]

Other examples of vindictive principals are found in the actions of elementary or middle school principals. Pressure to change grades is more common, but usually occurs behind closed doors. Also more commonplace than the public is aware, principals shun teachers that speak their minds. School leaders do not like teachers who are unafraid to work through a faculty association's grievance process on behalf of their personal safety, and the well-being of students. Such principals often refuse to recognize the existence of teachers who step up and demonstrate strength to the principal's weakness, overtly shunning the reporting teacher.

One specific example is the principal that is known to assign shunned teachers *the classes from hell*. This principal is known for having a memory from previous years and for practicing vendettas against teachers of previous years. She intimidates teachers with whom she has had run-ins by standing in the backs of classrooms, just watching, without uttering a word from her entry into the classroom until exit. These practices are childish and *should not* be part of a principal's actions. If there is an issue with a teacher, private meetings should be scheduled to address whatever issues exist.

Some faculty who have experienced some of these behavioral *should nots* by a principal have filed grievances. School leaders should be examples of leadership and not people of weak character who play favorites, practice small-minded vindictiveness, or participate in gossipy on-campus cronyism. These types of practices only diminish the respect of the position of administrator and drive teachers away.

The campus mood is often set by the campus leader. Administrators' actions *should not* be the reason for cultivating spirits of diminished morale and displays of hostility among faculty. They also should not allow parents or students to threaten the safety of teachers, while on the job. Students sense a weak leader, whether it is a teacher or school leader. No one really knows the extent of problems triggered on campuses by students, as a result of poor educational leadership.

In closing, teachers' associations and unions should lobby for language in their collective bargaining agreements that hold school-site or building principals accountable for the responses to cries for assistance. Time and time again, anecdotal reports come to light regarding weak school leadership and have led to a festering, negative campus culture and classroom toxicity. This is another reason students feel empowered over teachers and another reason teachers leave the profession.

The time has come to reverse this empowerment and elevate teachers to a more rightful position in American public schools. School leaders, whether given the title of administrator, principal, or instructional leader, can help to accomplish this. After all, are teachers not also entitled?

REVERSING THE TREND

The more tools teachers have in their instructional and classroom management tool kits, the better equipped they are in dealing with today's students. As with all equipment, the tools are only good if they are used. Unfortunately, there are far too many irrelevant educational supplements that are left untouched, once classroom routines are established.

There are a few essential classroom management strategies that are billed as effective toward classroom success for K–12 teachers. A good gauge for any strategy that is introduced as effective is whether the strategy helps teachers teach better and whether it improves student learning. Strategies that provide neither are a great source of frustration for teachers.

More often than not, bureaucrats are most concerned about the welfare of students, and minimize the importance of the teacher. The most unfortunate part is that sometimes teachers even reach the point of minimizing themselves as secondary. Teachers must be elevated to a higher status of respect in America.

Teachers tend to live by phrases that capture elements of educational philosophies. One of these phrases is *make no waves*. The problem with this phrase is that students do not adopt it for themselves. Hence the reason for teachers refining their classroom management strategies. Those recently placed in classrooms are more reluctant to speak up. Veterans closing in on retirement are normally counting the months. Those in the middle of their careers are facing choices as well, in terms of speaking up about concerns.

Students with special needs do require different discipline strategies. What they do not require is different treatment if it is determined that these students are violent, or habitually lash out, harming students and teachers. Bureaucrats must understand that political correctness is not a strategy of protection for teachers or students.

Effective classroom strategies could mean the difference between teachers staying in the profession or leaving. Although nothing in education is assured, teacher retention is best accomplished with strong administrative leadership. A strong and supportive administration that has solid professional learning communities and on-campus mentoring demonstrates that teachers are of prime importance.

NOTES

1. Dorothy Espelage, Eric M. Anderman, Veda Evanell Brown, et al. "Understanding and preventing violence directed against teachers." February–March 2013. *American Psychologist* 68, no. 2, pp. 75–87.
2. Don Matics. "Admins: Teachers to blame for student assault." *Fox 13 News*. April 28, 2017. Retrieved from http://www.fox13news.com/news/local-news/251513737-story.
3. Ibid.
4. Rose Eveleth. "Nineteen states allow teachers to spank children." *The Smithsonian Magazine*. February 19, 2014. Retrieved from https://www.smithsonianmag.com/smart-news/nineteen-states-allow-teachers-spank-children-180949810/.
5. Ibid.
6. Staff. "Tennessee school district looks to end corporal punishment." *Daily News*. October 23, 2017. Retrieved from https://www.memphisdailynews.com/news/2017/oct/23/tennessee-school-district-looks-to-end-corporal-punishment/.
7. Ibid.
8. Harold Pierce. "Districts reorganize disciplinary policies after 2014–2015 data." *The Bakersfield Californian*. October 24, 2017, p. 3.
9. Editors. "Q & A with Cheryl Ching." Fall/Winter 2017. *University of Southern California Rossier School of Education Magazine*, p. 25.
10. Robert J. Marzano. *Classroom management that works: Research-based strategies for every teacher*. 2003. Alexandria, VA: Association for Curriculum Development and Supervision, p. 13. See also Michael Linson. *The classroom management secret and 45 other keys to a well-behaved class*. San Diego, CA: JME, 2013.
11. Rob Plevin. *Take control of the noisy class: From chaos to calm in 15 seconds*. New York, New York: Crown, 2016.
12. Michael D. Simpson. "What NEA affiliates are doing to protect members from violent and disruptive students." July 12, 2017. *National Education Association*. Retrieved from http://www.nea.org/home/42238.htm.
13. Mark Keierleber. "Is DeVos near ending school discipline reform after talks on race, safety?" *The 74*. November 20, 2017. Retrieved from https://www.the74million.org/article/is-devos-near-ending-school-discipline-reform-after-talks-on-race-safety/.
14. Michael D. Simpson. "What NEA affiliates are doing to protect members."
15. D. Boyd, P. Grossman, M. Ing, et al. "The influence of school administrators on teacher retention decisions." 2011. *American Education Research Journal* no. 48, pp. 303–33. See also Staff. "Preventing violence against teachers." November 2013. *American Psychological Association Task Force* 44, no. 10. Retrieved from http://www.apa.org/monitor/2013/11/ce-corner.aspx. Italics added by author.
16. Lauren Foreman. "KHSD board to reassign Mira Monte principal." *The Bakersfield Californian*. June 5, 2015. Retrieved from http://www.bakersfield.com/archives/khsd-board-to-reassign-mira-monte-principal/article_57d44b73-391b-5f77-b2d2-44010caba987.html.

Chapter Five

Intervention, Training, and Retaining

Studies on teacher retention and attrition have suggested that more than 40 percent of all teachers leave the profession within their first five years, and that high-poverty, high-minority public schools have even higher rates of turnover.... Without specific strategies aimed at retaining these teachers, we may not change the current status quo, the exodus of top teaching talent. The good news is that our retention problem is fixable. Research into how to motivate and retain early career teachers indicates that they want leadership roles and dedicated time for teacher leadership. While some teachers are inherently committed to lifetime careers in teaching, for those on the fence, opportunities for leadership can make the difference.[1]

Funded by the U.S. Department of Education's Office of Special Education Programs (OSEP), the Technical Assistance Center on Positive Behavior Interventions and Supports (PBIS) supports schools, districts, and states to build systems capacity for implementing a multi-tiered approach to social, emotional and behavior support. The broad purpose of PBIS is to improve the effectiveness, efficiency, and equity of schools and other agencies. PBIS improves social, emotional, and academic outcomes for all students, including students with disabilities and students from underrepresented groups.[2]

Today's public school teachers wear many hats and take on many roles. Titles are assigned for these roles, such as instructor, classroom manager, and even content expert. However, another important role has been added: *Interventionist*. This is not a new role for teachers. It is now a role with an official title.

Frameworks and programs now exist that claim to be comprehensive in dealing with issues that include schools, families, and communities. The fact is that teachers have always intervened in schools, with students, colleagues, and families. Whether it is classroom dissension, or students refusing to learn, or even relationships between students, teachers tend to get involved.

Getting in the way of failure is an interventionist's necessity, if not his calling. These opportunities to affect students and the learning environment are now much more technical. As interventionists today, teachers are trained to go beyond their past practices and intuitions. If there is hope for the future, which can lead to the probability of retaining teachers, then maybe a multi-tiered intervention approach may be just the right incentive.

EVERY TEACHER AS AN INTERVENTION PRACTITIONER

In general, teachers by nature develop a brief personal philosophy for creating the most positive and safest learning environment for their students. Intervention does not begin when students become violent, or begin shouting obscenities in the classroom. Teachers must think through which students will be seated in the classrooms and begin to strategize how best to handle the what-ifs of the students prone to disruptions in the class.

If there is no advanced process of thinking through this initial positioning, then managing a classroom will be much more difficult on the fly. Teachers should incorporate into their roles as classroom teachers, and classroom managers, the role of interventionist in the following seven ways.[3]

1. *Consistency in what is said and done.* This is accomplished by clear establishment and fair application of classroom rules. Teachers should have short lists of rules that are possible to follow and enforce as learning experiences and are not for punitive retribution.
2. *Develop and apply some positive reward system* that enables student incentives and motivation. Avoid the fluff of over-complimenting and be careful not to set up a policy where everyone must be rewarded at all times. What students earn, students come to appreciate. This lesson will serve students well when they meet the real world of competition and employment. The best method is for students to adapt their own system of positive statements that is genuine and stems from intrinsic growth of character.
3. *Demonstrate genuine concern and an uncompromising support* for students' efforts in the present, and make every effort to point their efforts to a future context. Encouragement goes a long way. Pressing students to go one step farther enables risk-taking, which eventually demonstrates that failing is not failure. Rather, failing is one step closer to success, and such learning has validity for later in life. Teachers who are able to convince students that risk-taking for the

sake of learning can be fun and adventurous will be able to move the class in positive directions.

4. *Enable students to make choices from a set of good alternatives.* Students should be taught that there is not always one way to arrive at an answer, and that sometimes several vantage points produce the best answer. Students should learn to analyze and weigh the costs and benefits of choices by examining impacts of choices, upon themselves and upon others around them. Thinking critically and unselfishly is something that needs to be developed by today's students. The teacher can assist in modeling this approach. What students should come away with is that the respectful challenging of ideas, even though it might make them uncomfortable, is a good thing. Learning to disagree without hatred, violence, and name-calling is something we need to see more often. The adults of the nation could learn much from students that finally comprehend this and practice it.

5. *Stay abreast of mood changes in the classroom.* Teachers must gauge the *body language of the classroom*. The most effective teachers are aware of topics that students are passionate about, and monitor the growth and maturity of students in their understanding of the depths of these topics. The class, at the direction of the teacher, can discuss reasons why insults and violent protests are not good options when disagreement occurs. This also leads to safer classrooms for teachers and students.

6. *Work to diffuse the gathering emotions that are headed in the wrong direction.* Sometimes students do not let things go, especially when their emotions are involved. Teachers would do well to keep a witty and relaxed sense of humor at the ready. If there is a disagreement between teacher and student, and emotions escalate, the teacher should consider whether it is a battle worth fighting. When issues arise in the classroom that might pit a student against the teacher, have a de-escalation strategy upon which to call. For example, if a student is on the verge of an emotional outburst, find ways to de-escalate the emotion. It is always difficult to bring a student down from an emotional loss of self-control. Teachers can keep these moments from worsening. One method that is recommended is the crowd-friending model, which is addressed later in the chapter.

7. *Be flexible enough to let students know that changing something,* or accommodating an exception, is often part of life. Rigidity in the face of common sense and decency can lead to emotional reactions in short order. Today's students are more highly inclined toward a sense of fairness and are quick to apply emotions and expressions to demonstrate their feelings on matters. Gen Z bases their reality on these feelings, and less on facts and reason. So, they need to be taught the

rational approach as it relates to change that may appear unfair. This is a necessary life skill.

INTERVENTION PROGRAMS

Past intervention programs for American public schools focused on a few basic areas. Primarily these intervention programs had as their goals changing students' mindsets and limiting excessive behaviors. Along with these goals, the overall intent was for students to own their actions and reflect on them. Schools today would consider a behavior modification program a success if discipline referrals, suspensions and expulsions were down, after they applied the program. Those would be classified as positive responses to intervention.

Teachers are often natural problem-solvers, which means they are involved in intervention at some level through their skills in seeking solutions. What is interesting is that teachers are fed so many programs to implement that often the lifespan of any one program is short-lived. Due to changes in students, the daily necessities of academics, and overall classroom management, districts buy into something and then require teachers to apply it.

Sometimes programs can lack substance, seeking only to manipulate students' thinking and feelings. Other times a program can outlive its novelty. Who can forget the "character virtue of the week," where students were expected to focus on being honest one week, and somehow translate that into a second week, while continuing to demonstrate the previous week's respect for others?

Intervention Is Sometimes a Reaction

The majority of intervention programs are the result of reacting to problems that have become concerns for schools. Sometimes, an intervention is the result of factions seeking a form of equity, or tackling a problem associated with inequity, which became an issue from attention paid to one faction or another. Programs that elevate one group over another tend to separate rather than unite.

Intervention programs are rarely proactive. They are often more reactionary. For example, anti-bullying programs have sprung forth because of people suing schools on behalf of their children, who were being bullied by other students. Some of this bullying had led to students taking their own lives, which then led to suicide prevention programs and suicide awareness weeks in schools.

Breadth of Intervention

Similarly, counter-truancy programs, anti-smoking, and anti-drug and anti-alcohol programs exist in schools. There are also interventions for athletes to remain eligible to play sports, online school and classes for students to graduate, and even programs to assist the homeless, so they can attend school. Curiously, where are all of the programs for teachers to ward off violent students and parents? Changing students' mindsets doesn't necessarily hold up when emotions overrule minds.

Lawsuits also lead to changes on campuses ranging from exclusive clubs to reviews of school bathroom and locker room policies. Whether racial, ethnic, citizenship status, or special education-related, intervention programs have been developed and brought to the classrooms at all levels by law. These programs are usually pressed into practice, to the chagrin of some and to the joy of others.

When it comes to protecting factions of students at schools, laws are much more inclined toward favoring political or social factions than they are about protections for teachers. These laws result in unfortunate, unintended consequences for some intervention programs. Sometimes the laws and programs collide with each other and can cause additional conflict.

At both secondary and post-secondary institutions, safe-space intervention locations on campuses are places where allies are found to comfort those seeking solace. Safe spaces have been created as a reaction to emerging issues emanating from Generation Z's adjustments to violence directed at them, or as a result of the demographics that preceded them. One only wonders, as Gen Z teachers begin to dominate the classrooms, whether there will be a multitude of safe spaces for the teachers, created on campuses all over the nation.

Word of Caution

Schools have been criticized as places for social engineering, and there are claims that this *programming* has taken precedence over learning. As the argument goes, some state that teaching and learning are diminished as schools continue to expand as social agents. Others claim in order for students to learn, their basic needs must be first be met.

All of this is well and good, and students today do have needs on grander scales. But so do teachers! Most educators and parents seem to think of intervention as just getting between situations and solving them. There is some of that. But there is much more to intervention than a program to diminish behaviors or actions.

A LOOK AT PBIS TRAINING

Positive Behavioral Interventions and Supports is a multi-tiered framework that has as its ultimate purpose interventions into behaviors on school campuses. It is defined by scholars as "a framework for enhancing the adoption and implementation of a continuum of evidence-based interventions to achieve academically and behaviorally important outcomes for all students."[4]

As an intervention, PBIS has been around in different forms since the 1980s. The focus of intervention strategies evolved to where PBIS is today, as a comprehensive framework meant to be implemented. Two of the aims of PBIS are (1) to reduce in disciplinary referrals, suspensions, and expulsions among groups that have been underrepresented and (2) to improve the effectiveness, efficiency, and equity of schools.[5] Other aims include the application of strategies toward outcomes in social and academic areas.

Sugai and Simonsen write: "Schools that are effective in their implementation have (a) more than 80% of their students and staff who can indicate the desired positive behavioral expectations for a given school setting, (b) high rates of positive acknowledgements for contributing to a positive and safe school climate, (c) have more than 70–80 percent of their students who have not experienced an office discipline referral for a disciplinary rule infraction."[6]

PBIS, when used schoolwide, is intended to engage five separate systems comprehensively. These include: (1) School-Wide Systems, (2) Classroom Setting Systems, (3) Non-Classroom Setting Systems, (4) Individual Student Systems, and (5) Family Systems.

An estimated 20,000 public schools around the nation have had faculty trained in PBIS, and have adopted the PBIS framework and strategies. The framework includes support networks, schools, families, and communities, as well as training sessions, within which there are several tiers of support described. Along with the policies surrounding the program, and specifics on how to apply PBIS to high schools, families are expected to be engaged in the process to deal with bullying[7] and other issues.

There are four misconceptions about PBIS that are important to understand. First, PBIS is not an intervention program as such. It is a framework, as was mentioned earlier. As a framework, it is comprehensive in its application of features, all of which are based in research. A second misconception is that reward incentives characterize some sort of carrot for students who behave. In actuality, PBIS enables students to learn positive traits that are rewards in and of themselves.

The third misconception surrounding PBIS is that the framework was designed specifically for students with disabilities. While disabled students and others who have been underrepresented have a focal point in the framework, the framework is actually designed to be successful for all students in schools.

Finally, the fourth misconception is that PBIS is for behavioral modification, akin to other intervention strategies, such as the former Response to Intervention (RtI). The reality is that "the PBIS framework is the application of RtI principles to the improvement of social behavior outcomes for all students."[8] RtI has been renamed and is now a part of PBIS under the title of Multi-Tiered System of Support (MTSS), and it focuses "primarily on addressing academic problems . . . as the new way to think about both disability identification and early intervention assistance for the most vulnerable, academically unresponsive children in schools and school districts."[9]

DISCIPLINE AS INTERVENTION

There should be a difference between policy and procedures, in handling students who speak out of turn, and students who assault teachers and fellow students in the classroom. Keeping students in school at all costs, or sending them back to classes after there have been assaults, is just not the best approach. A student-signed behavior contract is not an effective tool, especially when students know there are few consequences when contracts such as these are broken time and time again.

A classroom policy that requires a violent student to be sent to the office, only to be sent back within minutes, is frustrating and demoralizing. Administrators who are in tune with teachers' policies are more apt to align their office disciplinary measures with the classroom management policy of the classroom teachers. PBIS should be for administrators as much as it is for teachers and students. But do administrators seek to discover which students may pose more problems than others?

Consistency in Discipline

Discipline should be consistent and, if used appropriately, can be used as in-class intervention to correct behaviors. Students who have very little self-discipline, and express violent behaviors, are a great challenge to the psychological health of other children. Each time they lash out they are also harming the educational process.

If violent students are going to be kept at school, then there should be a class into which they can be placed to work independently of others. This placement should be where education can still occur, but with a much lower ratio of teachers to students and an environment more understanding and tolerant of outbursts, should they occur.

The programs of discipline that are in place in many public schools come across as favoring the troubled students over the teachers. This is inequitable.

Such programs stress empathy toward students over empathy toward teachers. Troubled students kept in classrooms where other troubled students are on edge will eventually trigger some students to struggle with their own self-control issues. This type of discipline lacks consistency.

Removing a student from the classroom, either temporarily or permanently, sends many messages. Positive messages and actions let teachers know the administrator cares about him or her and the safety of all involved. This removal also demonstrates care for the education of the other troubled students, or those classified as special needs.

Nothing speaks more loudly in support of a teacher than an administrator who understands and acts accordingly to demonstrate this support. If students are to remain in classes and have a chance at stability, then the rest of the students who are not triggered may well assist in providing answers.

BEHAVIOR INTERVENTION STRATEGY: CROWD-FRIENDING

Students Avoiding Violence Effectively

Schools are hearing much about strategies meant to ward off violent behaviors in the classroom. Whether these behaviors are directed at students or teachers, they are still violent and need a response. Much has been made of "active shooter" responses, and rightly so. Any violence in schools is unacceptable. It should be obvious that not all violence that occurs at schools comes from without. Therefore, whether the violence is verbal or physical, it must be asked what is being done in classrooms to thwart the violence that comes from within?

Americans have heard the online term crowd-funding. Likewise, our culture is familiar with the concepts of crowd-sourcing and crowd-pleasing. Now we can also incorporate the term Crowd-Friending (CF). Crowd-friending is a tactic of planned student responses that can be utilized in many classrooms in all types of schools, but probably best in primary and middle schools. It is a practical strategy for *Students to Avoid Violence Effectively* (SAVE).

Due to the nature of actions of older students, the acts committed by those nearing adulthood should be handled differently. The crowd-friending strategy applied to elementary and middle school students has a much better chance of coming across as caring, and less provocative, more empathetic, and less invasive. Among high schoolers, the notion of crowd-friending might come across as escalating a situation, running the risk of increasing violent tendencies. The payoff would be that a program introduced early enough in a school, or district, would become a part of school culture and may reap benefits, ascending well into secondary classrooms.

CF can be added to existing frameworks of intervention, or used as an intervention strategy on its own. Students may come to view it as a positive, in terms of community building, and be proud of their ability to reduce behavioral outbursts in the classroom. One key to the strategy is not to use it every time one of the students has an incident. Therefore, both the students and the teacher could signal its usage.

The Strategy of Crowd-Friending

Essentially, CF works by engaging the potential violent actor with affirmations and overwhelming spoken comments of a positive nature, from all corners of the room. The intent of the positive comments is that the potential actor backs away from his or her actions by hearing the class involvement. This involvement is meant to distract the attention of the actor and divert potential behaviors.

If successful, the potential for violence may be lessened, or even thwarted. In order for CF to be effective, students and teachers must be aware of the classmates who have propensities to demonstrate anger and potential violence. In any classroom, these students manifest themselves in short order.

The classroom teacher or intervention strategist can run simulations in class with fictitious characters, or characters from literature, to automate responses. Even the school's principal can get involved as the student with the issue, as a role play. These simulations can include the entire class during times of peace, just for practice and student buy-in.

Of course, a teacher must be aware when CF is not working, and require students to resort to Plan B. Plan B means to "back down," or "bail to a safe place." A code word of the day can be used to de-escalate the class's responses accordingly.

This CF strategy can be applied when a student begins with verbally assaulting others, or begins to demonstrate other self-control issues. Caution should be exercised as certain emotionally disturbed students may tend to act out more aggressively if approached incorrectly.

Teachers should know their students well enough, including their backgrounds and previous issues in school, to shape the classroom environment towards de-escalation and safety. All things considered, if CF works in just a fraction of the time, then classrooms become safer places for teachers and students. Here is how it is proposed to be implemented.

Implementation of Crowd-Friending

The strategy plays out in the following fashion. Before, or at the beginning of, an outburst by a student known for such behavior, students in the *Zone of*

Immediate Proximity for Assault (ZIPA), use their understanding of their classmate's outburst to trigger positive responses. Students nearest the struggling student in question often hear or see the beginnings of frustration, so they recognize the student about to "go off."

The students in the zone, like all others who notice the same beginning or trigger behavior, have the teacher's permission in class to speak in a normal tone to the student who is struggling, by saying distractingly positive statements in normal, friendly voices. Then, in concentric fashion, other students use phrases to distract the student from his or her original struggle, and enlarge the conversation until the teacher can step in and call for assistance, or until the student's assigned aide can grasp the severity of the situation.

The concentricity of the students' positive statements is usually enough to defuse an angry classmate from an outburst, or delay something more serious, until assistance arrives. Positive peer pressure is nothing new. When done properly and caringly, the results can be amazing.

At the point of initial engagement, the responses should be standard for all students, and all students should be directed to respond in kind, regardless of the student struggling. If nothing else, the distraction enables the teacher to intervene, or call security or an administrator for assistance. In situations that tend to escalate quickly, every second of delay moves the environment closer to an outburst of violence. The use of CF early on means that every second there is a delay of the possibility of violence is a good second.

Crowd-friending can be used in many grade levels to shape classroom cultures. It allows students to own their environments and participate in their own safety, to a certain extent. CF should never be used as a last-ditch effort, or as a replacement for calls for security. CF should be naturally embedded in a classroom from the beginning of the year, which is why it can be used with many initial classroom disturbances, and not just those involving a history of acting out, or assaulting others.

Crowd-friending essentially is teaching what amounts to group regulation in the classroom. There is always more impact when peers, as a community, step forward to own their classroom. Students can begin to take ownership of the model by developing posters that fit the specific classroom environments.

The posters could be designed by students and placed around the classroom, to remind students of things to say when they need to step up and hold each other accountable. Administrators should consider encouraging the development of a CF-type program, or give CF a chance all by itself. Students are often the best regulators of their friends' behaviors, even if they find it difficult controlling their own. Teachers should feel free to adjust any of the above behavior modification strategy to the environment in which they work.

PROFESSIONAL DEVELOPMENT: TRAINING FOR TEACHERS WHO EXPECT TO WORK WITH GENERATION Z STUDENTS[10]

The call for professional development for teachers is being shouted from the rooftops, and the call must be answered. The following professional development is suggested as an excellent set of first steps toward educating new and veteran teachers about making good choices with student and work relationships. These good choices could lead educators toward a vibrant and prolonged career. Conversely, poor choices can lead to legal troubles and career and life ruination.

Each of the following professional development topics are suggested to be covered in sessions that include new teachers and veteran teachers. Since education is more about people than it is about content, the professional development topics are presented with people in mind. After each topic there is also included a brief statement pertaining to and emphasizing its' importance for the educator. Schools and districts should consider these topics *before* career-altering incidents occur.

Professional Development Topic 1: Boundaries and Barriers to Teacher-Student Relationships

Boundaries must exist between teachers and students. Some of these boundaries are natural, due to age, gender, or interest. Others are established as policies and adherence to them is a form of social contract between teachers and students. What are districts' policies about these relationships?

Professional Development Topic 2: Technology, Temptation, and Students

The ubiquity of technology and the apparent dependence of students upon their smartphones have put extra pressure upon schools. The explosiveness of social media, coupled with the teenage penchant for attention, are bringing new temptations to teenagers. Often these temptations play out in the classroom with online posts, either resulting in the need for new school and classroom technology policies, or resulting in disciplinary actions. Are there clear policies and consequences stated?

Professional Development Topic 3: Teenage Brains, Maturity, and Emotions

Anyone working in education understands well that students and their biologies are different each day. This is especially true in secondary education. Students make decisions while they are still in the midst of sorting out their individuality. They often lack the knowledge that their emotions are hyper-intense, and that their brains are often not wired up to understand unintended consequences and extenuating implications of their actions. Teachers must be made aware of these particulars.

Professional Development Topic 4: Relationships Between Teachers and Teenage Students

At this juncture, some very difficult issues may arise when discussing this topic. For example, a school may have just experienced a horrible situation that has affected the confidence, reputations, and morale of the school. The community may still be dealing with legal and emotional fallout from an inappropriate relationship between a teacher and student, or a coach and an athlete. Whatever the case, the law must be followed, and the difficult work of open and honest conversation about all that has happened, as well as the establishment of a proactive approach to safeguarding, is beneficial in the long-run.

Professional Development Topic 5: Social Networking and Relationships in a Digital World

Most newly hired faculty come from the Z and Millennial Generations and understand the dependency and importance of technology and its involvement in the daily lives of their students. However, the issues of social media and networking take on different aspects for the teacher. Considerable time should be committed to discussing the policies for teachers and their uses of social media, especially when it comes to sharing those spaces with students.

As teachers, the shift must be made toward understanding the different roles of social media, and developing methods to use classroom technology for educational purposes. Educators must not cross relational lines with students. The reality is that the emerging Z Generation is wired differently that the Millennial Generation. Relationships on social media, forged before being hired, may have to be reconsidered. The fact is that involvement in social media now takes on different roles for those who become educators.

Professional Development Topic 6: School Culture and Relationships

The wider purpose of a school often encompasses added social dimensions. These dimensions sometimes expand to include meeting the needs of students and their families. Exploring the various dimensions that comprise good relationships between students and teachers, between schools and families, and across the community is beneficial to the larger purposes of the school.

Educational professionals across the board should consider what comprises good relationships between colleagues, as well as in additional intraschool relationships. This type of discussion not only provides clarity of purpose, but also may prove to be a worthy endeavor for school accreditation visitations.

Professional Development Topic 7: Education Policy: Morality, Purpose, and Common Sense

Why do teachers choose their careers? What factors drive teachers toward excellence?

What may be compromised when teachers choose to engage in inappropriate relationships or abuse their students are both character and professional ethics. How would such choices hurt the community at large? Is it ever the place of a school administrator to share with his or her faculty that he perceives the development of inappropriate relationships?

Teachers, for the most part, take their craft very seriously. There is much to lose by one poor choice and much to gain by affirming and practicing good choices. This cannot be emphasized enough.

Professional Development Topic 8: Technology: Tools and Tactics

Changes in the cultural climate regarding sex have more than seeped into school classrooms. Some days it seems more like a deluge. A major concern is that sexual predators are fully aware of the utilities of technology and methods in accessing potential victims. However, along with this very serious issue, there is also the issue of how easy it is today to accuse someone of something completely false.

False allegations are devastating and can ruin lives. The United States is not alone in experiencing this phenomenon.[11] Teachers must exercise caution when posting personal items online. Online statements and images can be manipulated and crafted to allege something that is not at all taking place outside a fictionally based digital realm.

Part of the proactivity required today is for teachers to consider what to do if a colleague is falsely accused of something that could result in a loss of career. Such accusations could result in the destruction of one's family, and/or the ruination of a career and community reputation. What should be done if a colleague discovers another faculty member has assaulted a student physically, or sexually? Mandatory reporter laws must be followed.

The teacher should receive harsh punishment under the law. In some states, the laws should be revised to extend this harshness as a deterrent.

Also, hiring interns, who are closer to the ages of their students as teachers, should be reconsidered.

The establishment of boundaries is critical for success in today's classrooms. These boundaries must also include considerations and policies regarding communications' technologies, and participation of teachers and students on social media as friends. In an effort to establish and maintain boundaries, professional development must become part of school districts' training and teacher training institutions are recommended to include some of the topics in their credential classes. The health and well-being of school personnel, as well as students and families, is at stake.

TEACHER EDUCATION PROGRAM TRAINING

Teacher training programs are vital to the long-term success of teachers and subsequent classroom skills. Along with instruction, practice, internships, and mentoring, excellent teacher training must include strategies to address the concerns of possible violence that face teachers these days. Sadly, "it is likely that violence directed toward teachers within teacher preparation programs is not a prioritized area of professional development training. However, given the global prevalence of teacher victimization, it is possible that many preservice teacher preparation programs do not prepare teachers adequately as effective classroom managers."[12]

Investigate Violence Against Teachers

Teacher training that does not incorporate safety components and does not involve "what if" scenarios for candidates will run the risk of being criticized as irrelevant—and may even place teachers into risky situations. Teacher training institutions must inform and train candidates thoroughly.

Teacher candidates in interviews should be aware of the numbers of assaults that occur within school districts. In fact, there ought to be a registry ranking schools in districts, according to their reports of violence, both officially and anonymously. If made official, the safety ranking should be included in evaluating schools.

To date, "many teachers have been shocked by frequent violent occurrences in our nation's schools during recent years and the far-reaching implications of violence. Such acts of violence have gone beyond tragic and have left behind untold educational, emotional, financial and other costs. . . . It is likely that violence toward teachers has an impact on teacher recruitment and retention by discouraging potential educators from entering the field of education."[13]

In terms of violence against teachers, there "is a significant yet under-investigated problem in the United States that has profound implications for schooling, teacher retention, and overall student performance."[14] Viewing the issue from a prevention perspective, "it is necessary to identify the contextual and individual factors that allow violence directed toward teachers to occur in the first place."[15] It was after deeper investigations and examinations of problems associated with student violence that programs were developed to deal with the growing problem.

Education is good at playing catch-up in response to problems that have reared their heads in culture for some time. The time is right to consider a larger framework to deal with the larger school community and engage all stakeholders in lessening the risk of dangers at school and in the community.

Multi-Systems Approach to Training

Multi-systems approaches should also be multi-tiered in application, and desired effects should be made clear. This clarity should extend to (1) students, (2) teachers, (3) the designs of classrooms, (4) instruction by the teacher, (5) the overall programs and policies of intervention and discipline at the school level, (6) staff development programs, (7) involvement of the community, and (8) faith-based organizations and churches. The approaches should receive district-wide support. In addition, Allen lists six ways[16] that a community can "support teachers and schools with good morale."[17] These include:

- Having a supportive PTA or parent group
- Active parent volunteers
- Adopting a classroom
- Parents helping build parent communication
- Engaged student support team
- Supportive leadership

PBIS Training

As mentioned earlier, PBIS is one such multi-tiered framework that includes the former RtI intervention, initially for special needs and special education. As a cluster, regardless of the program selected, intervention training should extend to all school personnel and into the community, and involve the parents and families, whereby "School board members, as well as other community leaders and organizers, should use their influence to engage youth in positive activities."[18]

Any intervention program that claims to shape students' behaviors and mindsets, and seeks to stem serious issues associated with violence against teachers, yet is not reducing teacher assaults, is missing the mark. Espelage, Anderman, and Brown agree, "As U.S. schools are implementing schoolwide positive behavior support frameworks and other targeted violence prevention programs, we suggest that these efforts not only assess violence among students but also include violence directed at teachers as an outcome measure."[19] Sometimes the most positive behavior change comes by way of a negative feeling through being held accountable.

RETAINING TEACHERS

Retaining teachers is problematic for public education. Addressing the problem of teacher attrition requires an examination of at least six considerations. Among these issues is how to prevent student aggression and violence. Additionally, researchers suggest the following as starting points.[20]

- First, administrators, teachers, parents, and students need to recognize that the problem of school-based violence is everyone's problem and responsibility.
- Second, teacher preparation programs at colleges and universities need to address a broad array of theory and practice in classroom management strategies and to support realistic opportunities for field experiences in the classrooms throughout their programs, not just during student teaching, such that all educators must master classroom management requirements before a license for teaching is issued.
- Third, teachers' attitudes and classroom practices are variables that may impact some levels of aggression in the classroom, which, in turn, predict aggression toward teachers.
- Fourth, the nature of student–teacher interactions is highly influential in academic and behavioral performance, and conflictual relationships are predictive of aggressive tendencies on the part of both students and teachers.
- Fifth, school climate factors are highly influential in creating a context that facilitates or inhibits violence against teachers.
- Finally, undefined public spaces increase the likelihood of violence relative to other spaces that are defined (e.g., classrooms).

Training and retaining teachers is a major concern for every state. These concerns will persist into the near future. Issues that influence whether people will eventually enter the teaching profession, stay in the teaching profession for additional time, or leave the profession altogether should be concerns for all Americans.

Teachers Leaving the Profession

The numbers of enrolled students in teacher training institutions have decreased over the past several years. The numbers of teachers leaving the profession in the first three-to-five years have been increasing during this same time period. Teachers are retiring earlier than anticipated for a host of issues. Thus, states are grappling with what to do to reverse the trend.

According to Podolsky, Kini, and Bishop, et al., there are more than 200,000 teachers that leave the profession annually. The researchers suggest there are "five major factors, and related policies, that influence teachers' decisions to enter, stay in, or leave the teaching profession."[21]

These five major factors and subfactors[22] include (1) *financial issues with salaries, benefits and family needs*, (2) *the costs associated with paying for college to train in a school of education, which usually means the student cannot work*, (3) *issues of hiring and related personnel management issues after being hired*, (4) *the amount of support by colleagues and administration for those newer to the profession*, and (5) *the actual conditions of the teaching job*, (a) *including the principal*, (b) *whether there is time for professional development and collegial collaboration*, (c) *the question of how a teacher may hold students accountable*, (d) *professional learning communities involving many teachers for shared decision-making*, and (e) *the numbers of resources available to be able to teach well, including technology, textbooks, and supplies*.

Veteran teachers who have been around awhile have experienced the rebranding and repackaging of educational programs, which have promised to assist in elevating students in classrooms toward overall greater performance. These programs assure teachers that by applying them to classroom circumstances, students will be enabled to comply and become more productive academically.

This compliance, teachers are assured, would be behavioral, and evidenced by higher academic outcomes. The proponents of the programs assure teachers that their ideas are based in science and the literature backs them up. If this is true, then why do some teachers say they are leaving the profession for exactly the opposite outcomes? Are these just poor teachers?

Teachers Desire Professional Opportunities

If surveys are correct, then what teachers' desire is the possibility to advance in their careers without having to go the administrative route. McCann, Zuflacht, and Gilbert point out that teachers seek "Career ladder opportunities"[23] to grow into leadership roles in teaching. Those who prefer to remain in the classroom are seeking to grow into other dimensions of the profession. The three ways this could be accomplished are discussed below.

- Internal Opportunities for Leadership and Specialization: distinguished teacher roles; professional development leaders; content-area specialists
- Opportunities through Outside Organizations: teacher leadership in school success
- Restructuring Staffing and Scheduling for Improved Retention: differentiated teaching responsibilities; restructuring how personnel are used

Advantage Lost?

America is not as competitive in education as it once was. Far too many lawsuits favoring factions and individuals have gutted some of the incentives that have worked in the past. The forced equality of outcomes has diminished the quality of the condition of education, so much so that everyone receiving a diploma for graduating high school now realizes there is not much to celebrate over possession of their high school *trophy*. The requirement in the United States for gaining a high school diploma is showing up to class most days. This is reminiscent of recreational sports, where everyone receives something similar as a reward for participating.

THE CHALLENGES TO IMPROVING RECRUITMENT AND TEACHER RETENTION

The challenge to states and local communities under the ESSA is to develop a serious program that is cutting-edge and brings back authority to teachers.[24] This would be attractive to teachers entering the profession. Currently, this authority rests with bureaucrats. The fact that bureaucratic power has increased is another reason teachers leave the profession early.[25] As long as everyone insists that all children have the same access to everything, and outcomes are left to the decision makers and not the teachers and students, our nation will be lagging further and further behind.

The bottom line is that students rarely appreciate what they do not have to earn. This is generally the same with adults. Granting access to education benefits for troubled students without having the students earn them only enables empathy from bureaucrats, and what the bureaucrats do not understand is that their empathy causes student apathy. Do teachers really want to be in a profession that shines trophies and cannot hold students accountable for working hard to reach their graduation?

Incentives

There are at least four incentives[26] that are directly tied to attracting teachers to the profession. Any one of these four incentives might convince a person to shift gears and enter the teaching profession, or stay in the game.

First, under ESSA, states and school districts have access to pilot program funding to hire teachers for lower-income areas in the nation, students who are English learners, or students in special education.[27] Second, state governments should raise teacher salaries and benefits so that they are more competitive with the average middle-class salaries in the United States.[28] Third, in areas where housing is extremely expensive, states should raise salaries, provide low-cost housing for teachers, or provide incentive financial packages for teachers willing to work in cities that are very expensive.[29]

Lastly, state universities should finance a good portion of tuition and fees for students willing to be in education as a career.[30] In fact, states could provide the scholarship funds to the universities with a guarantee that teachers would serve a minimum of two years at the same job. Private enterprises should invest in training new teachers.

Strong, Supportive Administrators

The education research on the connection between the administrator, or site principal, and school climate is abundantly clear. Administrators must find ways to do more to keep teachers at their schools. If this means speaking out at board meetings then that is what has to happen. Intervention for teachers is very important. Accordingly, "Really strong leadership by the administration is needed to create a positive learning climate. How well does the administration connect with the teachers, how well do they know the student? The entire ecology of the school and the community has to be taken into account."[31]

Strong, involved leaders can help to minimize student violence and support teachers who have already experienced workplace trauma. Jason Allen of *EdLanta* agrees: "As a classroom teacher, having the support of my Principal meant a lot. It helped me to grow into the Educator that I am today. My Principal understood that elevating and supporting teachers ensured that children would learn."[32]

Teacher Support Systems

Teachers' support systems need to be strengthened. If a teacher is assaulted by a student or parent while on the job, there are remedies that can be brought on behalf of the teacher. Teachers are "entitled to collect workers' compensation for damages, medical expenses, and lost pay, but most WC laws also preclude employees from suing their employers. But employees usually can sue the student (and his parents)."[33] Many would agree today that legal interventions may be the only way to go in some of the more egregious cases of assault against teachers.

Local Teachers' Associations

Teachers who are members of the *National Education Association* can have their local associations step forward to work through issues that occur. The following possible solutions exist as means of recourse for teachers.[34] Local associations can bargain collectively and use specific language in their CBAs, which recognizes the need for safer environments for employees. The main goal is to keep teachers in the classrooms. This also can include the necessity to feel safe from threats from students and parents while on the job.

- Should the administrator or building principal be negligent, or fail to take action on behalf of the teacher by removing the threat, then the teacher and the association liaison can file an official grievance with the district. One of the reasons for filing a grievance is the return of the student to class, after an administrator has been informed of the assault, or assaults.
- The teacher's association should make every effort to lobby the district and the school.
- Site principals should engage in discussion that would result in professional development and in-service. These should focus directly on how to deal with students who are within special needs categories, others that cause regular disruptions, and those who demonstrate volatility or violent tendencies or behaviors.
- Public school teachers have access to the National Education Association's Network. This network includes a Safe Schools Program, which contains links and information that, among other things, contains tips for school faculty and staff in dealing with violence and stress caused by assaults and school violence.

Lobbying for Changes in Laws

Worker's compensation laws that apply to school teachers, administrators, and other district/school employees should be changed to allow schools and principals to be sued for injuries incurred while on the job, if there is a clear act of negligence that is involved. Without this recourse, principals have no fear of placing high-risk students and previous violent offenders back into classrooms as quickly as possible to make their schools look good. School administrators should be able to pass the pressure on up the administrative ladder to those in the hierarchy above them.

Safety will improve significantly when accountability for administrators also improves. Maybe it is time to consider acts of violence against teachers with the same import as schools' graduation rates. Schools of quality should also be judged by their records of safety for teachers and students. Some even argue for school accreditation to be tied to school safety.

Often, the best intervention is an exciting classroom full of learning. Teachers should arrive at work "excited and motivated daily. Most importantly, they have to want to be at work."[35] How many teachers do not like their work because they are not meant for teaching, have poor administrators, or are not receiving any help for intervention? However, excellent teachers need help too. In reality, "People do their best when the atmosphere is conducive to learning and progress."[36]

REVERSING THE TREND

Intervention training is being used to empower teachers and to stem the exodus of teachers from public school classrooms in America. Other nations have found similar results by empowering teachers. The concept of intervention comes packaged primarily with programs geared for student interactions. Whether it is behavior modifications or focusing on aspects of student emotional learning through their affect, teachers are expected to be proficient in whatever intervention is adopted by their states and districts.

Today's teachers must be proficient in intervention strategies to be able to deal with troubled students, angry parents, and those whose behaviors lead to additional classroom concerns that stunt academic achievement. Several comprehensive intervention programs bill themselves as holistic in their effectiveness, in terms of dealing with all sorts of school-related and community-related issues.

Intervention programs should not be used *reactively*. Whether PBIS or SEL, it is incumbent on today's teachers to understand the nuances of each program and when to apply its principles. Teachers who are not part of the thousands of districts that have adopted intervention programs may be ill-prepared to handle the major issues of violence and special needs outbursts in their classrooms.

As illustrated in this chapter, crowd-friending is a strategy that can result in team-building, classroom environment ownership by students, and lead time for teachers to deal with emerging problematic situations in classrooms. The opportunity to intervene may also deter the need for a student to be sent to the office for discipline. CF is meant to be implemented as one strategy of many. Such tools developed by teachers, for teachers, may add to the longevity of a career in education.

Providing teachers with information about problem students, coupled with professional development for problems they may face in their classrooms before they occur, is a positive move. An overt strategy to maximize support for teachers is a strong signal that there is consideration given to reversing the trend of the teacher exodus from our schools.

NOTES

1. Colleen McCann, Sasha Zuflacht, and Tierra Gilbert. "The decade-plus teaching career." *Teach Plus*. n.d. Retrieved from http://www.teachplus.org/sites/default/files/publication/pdf/decade-plus_final.pdf.
2. "Positive Behavioral Interventions and Supports (PBIS)." *Office of Special Education Programs*. n.d. Retrieved from https://www.pbis.org/.
3. Dorothy Espelage, Eric M. Anderman, Veda Evanell Brown, et al. "Understanding and preventing violence directed against teachers: Recommendations for a national research, practice, and policy agenda: American Psychological Association board of educational affairs task force on classroom violence directed against teachers." *American Psychological Association*. 2016. Retrieved from http://www.apa.org/education/k12/teacher-victimization.pdf.
4. George Sugai, Robert H. Horner, Glen Dunlap, et al. "Applying positive behavioral support and functional behavioral assessment in schools." 2000. *Journal of Positive Behavioral Interventions* 2, no. 3, pp. 131–43.
5. "Positive Behavioral Interventions and Supports (PBIS)."
6. George Sugai and Brandi Simonsen. "Positive behavioral interventions and supports: History, defining features, and misconceptions." Monograph. University of Connecticut. 2012. Retrieved from http://www.pbis.org/common/cms/files/pbisresources/PBIS_revisited_June19r_2012.pdf.
7. Ibid.
8. Ibid.
9. "Multi-Tiered System of Support (MTSS) & PBIS." *Office of Special Education Programs*. n.d. Retrieved from https://www.pbis.org/school/mtss.
10. Ernest J. Zarra, III. "Addressing appropriate and inappropriate teacher-student relationships: A secondary education professional development model." 2016. *CLEARvoz Journal* 3, no. 2, pp. 15–29. Retrieved from http://journals.sfu.ca/cvj/index.php/cvj/article/view/26/29.
11. Tom Rawstorne. "Ruined by the lies of children: The teachers destroyed by the false allegations of pupils who know they're untouchable." *Daily Mail*. July 19, 2009. Retrieved from http://www.dailymail.co.uk/news/article-1200746/Ruined-lies-children-The-teachers-destroyed-false-allegations-pupils-know-theyre-untouchable.html.
12. Espelage, et al. "Understanding and preventing violence directed against teachers."
13. Ibid.
14. Ibid.
15. Ibid.
16. Jason B. Allen. "Teacher morale impacts achievement." *EdLanta*. December 8, 2017. Retrieved from http://edlanta.org/teacher-morale-impacts-achievement/.
17. Ibid.
18. Espelage, et al. "Understanding and preventing violence directed against teachers."
19. Ibid.
20. Ibid.
21. Anne Podolsky, Tara Kini, Joseph Bishop, et al. "Solving the teacher shortage: How to attract and retain excellent educators." *Learning Policy Institute*. September 15, 2016. Retrieved from https://learningpolicyinstitute.org/product/solving-teacher-shortage-brief.
22. Ibid.
23. McCann, Zuflacht, and Gilbert. "The decade-plus teaching career."
24. Ernest J. Zarra, III. *Common sense education: From Common Core to ESSA and beyond*. 2016. Lanham, MD: Rowman & Littlefield, pp. 31–35.
25. Ibid., pp. 72–77.
26. Podolsky et al. "Solving the teacher shortage."
27. Ibid.
28. Ibid.
29. Ibid.
30. Ibid.
31. Tim Walker. "Violence against teachers—an overlooked crisis." *NEA Today*. February 19. 2014. Retrieved from http://neatoday.org/2013/02/19/violence-against-teachers-an-over

looked-crisis-2/.
32. Allen. "Teacher morale impacts achievement."
33. Michael D. Simpson. "When educators are assaulted: From the NEA Office of General Counsel." *NEA Today*. March/April 2011. Retrieved from http://www.nea.org/home/42238.htm.
34. Ibid.
35. Allen. "Teacher morale impacts achievement."
36. Ibid.

Index

accountability, xviii
Adams, Jane Meredith, 23
ACLU, 36
ADD, 23
ADHD, 15
administrators, 9, 18, 77, 80; accountability, 104; blaming teachers, 11; constrained leadership, 80; creating positive learning climate, 103; distant, 78; effective, 78; fearful, 67; forgotten, 77; ignorance, 77; standards, 11; supportive, 78, 92, 103; unsupportive, 59; weakened, 10, 80
African-American. *See* black
Allen, Jason, 103
Alverta B. Gray Schultz Middle School, 51
American culture, 6
Anderman, Eric M., 99
AntiFa, 60
assault, 5; report of, 12; traditional American culture, 7
augmented reality, 47
autism, 15

Baby Boomers, xiii
Baltimore City teachers, 47
Baltimore County Schools, 47
behavior management strategies, 65; primary elements, 65; secondary elements, 65, 71; tertiary elements, 65
behavior modification, xviii

Benner, Aaron, 17
Bishop, Joseph, 101
black, 16, 17, 37; principal, 48; students, 69; teachers, 17
Bloomfield, New Jersey, xv
Bradshaw, Wendy, 9
brains: excited, 47; student, 12; traumatic effects, 47
broken system, 31
Brown, Veda Evanell, 100
bullying, 3
bureaucracy, 26, 36, 38, 39, 41, 69
bureaucrats, xviii, 4, 5, 9, 28, 32, 33, 35; blamed, 102; decisions, 71; diminish classroom management, 69; fear of action, 33; fear of fallout, 69; lack understanding, 14; legal attention, 69; lines established by, 28; need to understand, 38; obstruct, 13; standards, 11; time for action, 35

California, 3, 23, 50, 69, 70; associate superintendent of educational services, 56; *California's History-Social Science Curriculum Framework and State Standards*, 6, 35; California Teachers Association (CTA), 23, 24; educational code, 56; school districts, 78; self-esteem movement, 60; teachers, 24, 48
change, 60
Cheltenham High School, 6

Ching, Cheryl, 70; funded by Bill and Melinda Gates Foundation, 70; doctoral dissertation, 70
Clark, Adam, 56
classroom, xviii; atmosphere of learning, 105; behavior, xviii; challenges, 66; changes, 77; discipline, 46; displays of empathy, 74; management strategies, xviii, 11, 47, 65, 74, 75, 83; structure as triggers, 75; toxicity, 82
college, 30
Columbus, Ohio, 14
Common Core State Standards, 9, 35, 49, 59, 71, 73
common sense, 38, 43, 59
Como High School, 4
corporal punishment, xviii, 67, 68; nineteen states allow, 67; paddling, 67; spanking, 68; Tennessee reconsidering, 68; threat of, 68
Critical Race Theory (CRT), 16–17
Crowd-Friending Behavior Intervention Strategy (CF), 92, 105; elementary schools, 92; implementation, 93–94; middle schools, 92; plan B, 93; positive statements, 94; posters, 94; secondary schools, 92; simulations, 93; strategy, 93; Students Avoiding Violence Effectively (SAVE), 92; tool to assist, 105; Zone of Immediate Proximity for Assault (ZIPA), 94

Delaware Department of Education, 37
Democratic voters, 28
discipline policy, 55; as intervention, 91; consistency, 91; failure, 55, 56; race-based, 61; unwritten, 55
disparate impact theory, 15
Dolores Huerta Foundation, 36
Drake, Tom, 40, 41

economics, 48
EdLanta, 103
education, xviii; change, 71; codes, 56; crisis, 60; elite K-12, 72; entitlements, 12; equity, 23, 24, 38, 67, 70; local control, 8; marginalized, xviii, 45, 46, 60; professionals, 35; public, 38; shifts quickly, 71; soul of, 59

Egan, Candice, 53–54
Ekblad, John, 4
emotions, 89
empathy, 91; for students, 92; for teachers, 92
entitlement, 45
equity, 70
Espelage, Dorothy, 100
Every Student Succeeds Act (ESSA), 6, 8, 9, 35, 59, 73, 102, 103
Essex Fells, New Jersey, xv
Evangelical Christian, 39
Eveleth, Rose, 68
expulsions, mandatory, xviii
extreme intolerance, 39

fake news, 40
false allegations, 2; physical, 2; sexual, 2; vindictive, 2
families, 59
Federal Court (7th Circuit), 30
Ferrell, Elisa, 40
fights, 6
Florida, 67; Pinellas County, 67; Pinellas Classroom Teachers Association, 67
Fulmer, Kathleen, 52

Gandolfo, Mike, 67
gender, 7, 36
Generation Z, 12, 32; as teachers, 79, 89; adjusting to violence, 89; career choices, 79; compliance, 79; emotional gratification, 73; entering the workforce, 79; self-adulation, 73; self-benefit, 73; teacher shortages, 79; tolerance, 79; wired differently, 96
Gilbert, Tierra, 101
Government Accountability Office, 32
grade tampering, 48

Hamilton County, Tennessee, 68
Harrisburg, Pennsylvania, 47
Healey, Charles, 51
Health Information Network, 59
Hein, Eric, 24
Hempstead, New York, 51
high school diploma, 102
high stakes assessments, 73
Hispanic students, 36, 69

history revisionism, 73
housing for teachers: expense, 3; shortage, 3
Huntsville, Alabama School District, 40

inclusion, 23, 32
Indiana State Teachers Association, 52
inequity, 26
Instagram, 5
Internet, 5, 6
intervention, 24, 89; as reaction, 88; breadth of, 89; programs, 36, 105; strategy, 33; training, 37

justice: professional, 11, 12; social, 11; victories, 37

Kern High School District, 69
Kini, Tara, 101

Latinx, 70
lawsuits, 89
legislators, 35
lobbyists, 38
litigious society, 33
Los Angeles, 48

Madison, Wisconsin, 50; Madison Teachers Incorporated (MTI), 50; Temporary Restraining Order (TRO), 50; successes in court, 50
Massachusetts Teachers Association (MTA), 29, 51
McCann, Colleen, 101
McKenzie, Annika, 51
Mecklinburg High School, 6
mental health professionals, 24
merry monarch, 26
Michigan Supreme Court, 52
mindsets, 89
Minnesota, 4, 52, 53, 55; legislation, 52–53; State Senator Dave Brown, 52
Muslim culture, 39

National Center for Education Statistics, 47
national sins, 73
No Child Left Behind (NCLB), 8, 49, 73

National Education Association (NEA), 58, 59, 79, 104
new cultural paradigm, 28
Newtown, Connecticut, xii
New York, 4, 25; Board of Education, 26; codes of conduct, 25
North Carolina, 6

Obama Administration, 15, 38, 80; mandates, 80; quotas, 80
Occupational Safety and Health Administration, 41
Okeechobee Achievement Academy, 31
Olympics, 2018, x
one-size-fits-all, 35

parent, 25, 28; arrested, 51; bulldozers, 28, 32; power, 32; strangulation, 51–52; teach self-control, 25
Parkland, Florida, x, xii
penal systems, 55
personnel issues, 70
Philadelphia, Pennsylvania, 6
Podolsky, Anne, 101
police, 32
politicians, xviii, 33, 69; fear of action, 33; time for action, 35; agenda, 49
Positive Behavior Interventions and Supports (PBIS), 85, 90, 105; achieving outcomes, 90; for administrators, 91; improve efficiency of schools, 90; improve equity of schools, 90; misconceptions, 90–91; multi-tiered support system, 90, 91; reducing discipline issues, 90; ultimate purpose, 90
prison, 57
professional development, 59, 95; boundaries and barriers, 95; education policy, 97; school culture, 96–97; social networking, 96; teacher-student relationships, 96; technology and temptation, 95; technology tools, 97–98; teenage brains and maturity, 95
professional learning communities, 83
progressive policies, 10
psychotherapy, 25
public schools : restoration of position, 83; trouble, 3, 26

race, 16; baiters, 16; policy based on, 36; grading by, 49
Race to the Top, 73
racism, 16; accusations, 16; real, 16; compensation, 17
racist, 15
Rawlings, Mark, 4
Redford, Robert. *See The Way We Were*
re-immersion programs, 36
re-matriculation, 54
reputations ruined, 5
restorative justice, 24, 41, 54, 55
reversing the trend, 18, 41
rigor, 17
Rolling Hills Elementary School, 40

safe place, 12
Safe Schools Program, 59
San Francisco, 47, 48
School Boards Association Survey, 3
school : accommodations, 15, 26; boards, 39, 76, 80; discipline strategy, 76; enrollment, 3; high, 75; middle, 75; principals, 69; psychologists, 32, 33, 34, 35; shooting, x; social engineering, 89; violence, 32, 39, 65
school-site administrators/leaders, 80; cliques, 81; consistent behaviors, 82; establish campus mood, 82; hostility, 82; inform faculty and staff, 80; negativity, 81; open-minded, 81; speak privately with teachers, 80; support, 81; teacher authority, 80; uphold levels of respect, 82; vindictiveness, 81; violence, 81
sexuality, 36
Simonsen, Brandi, 90
skin color, 69
smartphones, 53, 68
Snapchat, 5
social, 60; experimentation, 60; justice, 4, 16, 41, 54; media, 5, 6, 16; militancy, 60; service professionals, 35; skills, 24
sociocultural changes, 7, 36
socioeconomic problems, 8
socio-edu-dysiac, 73
Social Emotional Learning (SEL), 60, 68, 105
soft, xiii; administration, xiii; targets, xii

Spokane, Washington, 8
St. Louis, Missouri, 6
St. Paul, Minnesota Public School District, 17, 53
Straub, Kevin, 6
Streisand, Barbra. *See The Way We Were*
stroke, 6
students: accommodations, 28–29; accountability, 10; accusations, 28; aggression, 28; arrests, 51; assailants, 42; autistic, 52; behaviors, 25, 46; bipolar, 35; centrism, 26, 27, 28; challenges to learning, 72; classifications, 14; consequences, 47; dethroned, 33; development, 47; discipline record, 55; disorders, 8, 66; emotions, 66, 75; expulsions, 24, 39, 49, 51, 51–52, 52, 56; factions, 89; fights, 14; frustration levels, 9; IEP, 28–29, 29; lack of self-control, 26; literacy rates, 49; mainstreamed, 57; marginalized, 61; mean-spirited, 34; minority referrals, 38; motivation, 74; profiling, 38; receiving a diploma, 49; risk factors, 35; safe spaces, 89; safety, 56; second chances, 77; self-regulation, 25; sent back to class, 78; severely disabled, 34; soft treatment, 61; special education, 14, 18, 31, 103; special needs, 11, 14, 15, 18, 28, 31, 32, 34, 39, 55, 66; special protections, 18; suspensions, 24, 39, 49; threats, 4; triggers, 33; violent, 11, 32, 34, 39, 54, 66; work modifications, 29
Sugai, George, 90
Supreme Court, 7, 36

teacher. *See* teachers
teacher education, 46; candidates, 46; investigate violence in schools, 98–99; long-term success, 98; multi-systems approach, 99; PBIS, 99; programs, 3, 46, 98; training, 8
teachers, 18, 35; assaulted, 70; attacked, 6; attrition, ix, xii, 3, 85; black, 17; blaming of, 10, 18; burnout, x; changes in laws, 104; collective bargaining, 58; dedicated, 46, 66; demoralized, 76; disciplinary concerns, 8;

disenchantment, 7; drowning in assessments, 34; economic reasons, 3, 103; emergency credential, ix, 26; exemplars, 30; expected to perform miracles, 34, 35; factors for leaving, 101; false allegations against, 97; feel unsupported, 78; fighting back, 58; frustration, 56; Generation Z, xi, 27; going the extra mile, 56; grade level facilitators, 72; held in esteem, 28; higher status, 83; housing, 48; humiliated, 76; idealism, 66; inappropriate behaviors, 27; incentives, 102; injury, 6; interventionist, 85, 86, 86–88; kicking of, 4; leaving profession, ix, 1, 3, 9, 47, 66, 101; live by phrases, 83; local teachers associations, 104; longevity, 105; marginalized, 46, 59; Millennials, xi; non-credentialed, ix, 26; opportunities for leadership, 85; passion, 59; prime importance, 83; problem solvers, 88; professional opportunities, 101–102; protections, 11, 50; resignations, 8, 9, 48; resilience, 72, 75; retirements, 2, 7; retention, 3, 19, 25, 85, 86, 100; reversing teacher exodus, 105; rights, 58; ruin career, 97; self-defense, 76; shaming, 18, 48; shortages, ix, 7; solving teaching shortage, 100; soulful callings, 18; standards, 11; student interns, 7; substitute, 6; support systems, 103; unconditional acceptance, 66–67, 67; unions, 4; use social media, 8; welfare, 68; worker's compensation, 104

Texas, 50
The Way We Were, 72
traditional marriage, 7, 36
traditional relationships, 36
Trump Administration, 80
Trump, Donald, 39

United Kingdom, 6
United States, 6, 26, 39, 60; blaming, 73; Department of Education (DOE), 85
University of Southern California Center for Urban Education (CUE), 70

violence, 5, 12, 14, 17; against teachers, 68; exposure, 47; tolerated, 47; forms, 5; multi-systemic problem, 65; outbursts, 12; recipients, 5; school, 5; student-caused, 32; teacher-directed, 30; threats, 30; triggers, 17; witnessing, 15
virtual reality, 47

whole child, 12
workers' compensation, 52

zero-tolerance, xviii, 31, 54, 56, 57; arguments for, 57–58; arguments against, 57, 58
Zuflacht, Sasha, 101

About the Author

Ernest J. Zarra, III teaches college preparatory U.S. government and politics and economics classes to seniors at the state-decorated and top-ranked Centennial High School in Bakersfield, California. Zarra has earned five degrees and holds a PhD in teaching and learning theory from the University of Southern California, with cognates in psychology and technology. He is a former Christian College First-Team All-American soccer player, former teacher of the year for the prestigious Fruitvale School District, and was awarded Top Graduate Student in Education from the California State University at Bakersfield.

Dr. Zarra has written eight books, including the following Rowman and Littlefield publications: (1) *Assaulted: Violence in Schools and What Needs to be Done* (2018), (2) *The Entitled Generation: Helping Teachers Teach and Reach the Minds and Hearts of Generation Z* (2017), (3) *Helping Parents Understand the Minds and Hearts of Generation Z* (2017), (4) *Common Sense Education: From Common Core to ESSA and Beyond* (2016), (5), *The Wrong Direction for Today's Schools: The Impact of Common Core on American Education* (2015), and (6) *Teacher-Student Relationships: Crossing into the Emotional, Physical, and Sexual Realms* (2013). His book *The Wrong Direction for Today's Schools* was the award-winning *2016 Choice Outstanding Academic Title*.

Zarra has written more than a dozen professional journal articles, developed curriculum, and served as a professional development leader and facilitator for the largest high school district in California, the Kern High School District. He also assists school districts as an educational consultant, leads seminars on classroom management and instructional methods, and presents at professional education conferences. He is a member in good standing of the *National Education Association, California Teachers Association*, the

Association for Supervision and Curriculum Development, American Educational Research Association, and several national honor societies, including *Kappa Delta Pi*.

Ernie is originally from Bloomfield, New Jersey, and is married to Suzi, who is also an educator. They have two adult children and have resided in California most of their adult lives.

www.ingramcontent.com/pod-product-compliance
Lightning Source LLC
Chambersburg PA
CBHW030143240426
43672CB00005B/255